Name : _____

P9-EDJ-673

Children's Illustrated Atlas

UNITED STATES

Editors
Anne Ford
Brett Gover
Nathalie Strassheim

Writers
Lynnette Brent
Leslie Morrison
Glen Phelan
Judy Smart Plumb

Illustrators
Susie Cooper (leaves, page 66)
Robert Hynes/Mendola Artists
Dave Henderson (page 72 & 73)/
Mendola Artists

Cartography
Robert K. Argersinger
Gregory P. Babiak
Barbara Strassheim Benstead
Marzee Eckhoff
Susan K. Hudson
Nina Lusterman
David Simmons
Thomas Vitacco

Photo Credits
(l=left, r=right, c=center, t=top, b=bottom)
© Gene Ahrens, 68 (Delaware Water Gap)
© American Stock, 15 (b c)
Archive Photos: © Jeff Greenberg, 17 (c r), 27 (c), 29 (c r), 37 (c l), 47 (t l), 51 (c l), 59 (c), 69 (t l), 85 (c), 93 (Crockett), 101 (Arlington)
© Tom Bean, 38 (c r), 76 (b l)
California Division of Tourism: © Robert Holmes, 18 (t r), 19 (t l)
© Cheyenne Frontier Days, 109 (rodeo)
Color-Pic Inc.: © Dr. E. R. Degginger, 10 (t l)
Bruce Coleman, Inc.: © Eric Horan, 88 (b r)
Corbis: © Tom Bean, 63 (b l), 79 (c l), © Annie Griffiths Belt, 54 (b l); © Bettmann, 55 (c l), 63 (b c); © Jonathan Blair, 108 (refinery); © Layne Kennedy, 36 (t r); © Buddy Mays, 57 (b r); © Kevin R. Morris, 43 (b c); © David Muench, 37 (b r); © The Purcell Team, 101 (b l); © Charles E. Rotkin, 93 (c l); © Richard Hamilton Smith, 107 (t l); © UPI/Corbis-Bettmann, 11 (c r), 13 (Kasson and Balto), 53 (b l), 71 (c l)
© Culver Pictures, 105 (c r), 107 (Ringling Bros. poster)
© Delaware Tourism Office, 25 (b l)
FPG International: © Laurence B. Aiuppy, 60 (t r); © James Blank, 108 (b r); © Jerry Driendl, 26 (t r); © Bob Glander, 84 (t l); © Telegraph Colour Library, 64 (c l); © Ron Thomas, 66 (b l)
First Image West: © Jim P. Garrison, 77 (b r)
David R. Frazier Photolibrary: © Trent Steffer, 32 (potato)
© Allen Fredrickson, 27 (b r)
© Rob Gallagher, 67 (Old Man of the Mountain color inset)
© Gary Irving, 98 (b l)
H. Armstrong Roberts: © H. Abernathy, 36 (b l), 47 (b r), 58 (b l), 78 (b l), 80 (Spring Frog), 90 (b); © G. Ahrens, 71 (b r); © J. Blank, 10 (t r); © Linda Burton, 66 (b r); 106 (b r); © F. Sieb, 56 (b r); © George Hunter, 17 (t l); © J. Irwin, 29 (b l); © R. Kord, 82 (b r); © Hiroyuki, 92 (b r)
Idaho Department of Commerce: © Kevin Simms, 32 (t r)
Image Bank: © Patti McConville, 68 (Princeton)
Index Stock: 72 (b r), 100 (b r); © Everett C. Johnson, 42 (b r); © Todd Powell, 97 (t l)
Liaison Agency: © Daniel J. Cox, 61 (c r); © Futran Photography, 102 (c r); © Hulton Getty, 11 and 29 (Martin Luther King, Jr.), 41 (c l), 81 (c r), 65 (c l); © Brian Smith, 22 (b r)
© Zig Leszczynski, 88 (c r)
© Jack McConnell, 22 (t r)
© David McCutcheon, 60 (t l)
© Mississippi Department of Archives & History, 57 (c l)
© David Muench, 58 (Alley Roller Mill), 64 (bristle-cone), 65 (b r), 96 (b r), 99 (b r)
National Geographic Society: © Melissa Farlow, 26 (b r), © Charles Nye, 105 (t l)
© Nebraska Department of Economic Development, 62 (b r)
© Joseph Nettis, 25 (c l)
© N.H. Division of Parks and Recreation/Dick Smith, 67 (Old Man of the Mountain B/W)
North Wind Picture Archives: 10 (b l), 11 (b c), 16 (b l), 18 (b l), 19 (c), 20 (b l), 21 (c), 22 (b l), 23 (c r), 23 (c r and train), 24 (t l), 26 (b l and b c), 28 (b r), 30 (b l and b r), 31 (c), 32 (Lewis and Clark), 33 (c l), 34 (b r), 35 (b l), 36 (b r), 38 (b l and b r), 41 (b l and b r), 42 (b l), 43 (c), 44 (b l), 45 (c), 47 (c l), 48 (b l and b r), 49 (c l), 52 (b), 56 (b l), 59 (c l), 60 (Lewis and Clark), 61 (c and b l), 62 (Lewis and Clark), 67 (b l), 68 (Hudson, Morse), 69 (b r), 73 (c r), 75 (c), 76 (b r), 78 (fort), 82 (b and b l), 83 (c r), 84 (seal of Penn's colony, signing of Declaration of Independence, and b r), 87 (b l), 88 (Jackson, Ft. Sumter), 91 (c l), 92 (Jackson), 97 (c r), 98 (b), 99 (t l), 100 (b l), 101 (Jefferson), 102 (Lewis and Clark), 104 (b), 106 (Nicolet), 108 (fort, train), 109 (b r); © Nancy Carter, 77 (c l)
© Frank Oberle, 58 (t r)
© Ohio Division of Travel and Tourism, 78 (t r)
© Oklahoma Tourism, © Fred W. Marvel, 80 (b r)

© Laurence Parent, 46 (b l), 81 (c l)
© PhotoDisc, 5 (flag), 18 (Rte. 66 sign), 19 (t l), 28 (peanuts), 45 (saxophone), 54 (snowshoes), 74 (spool), 86 (seagulls), 92 (banjo), 96 (boots)
PhotoEdit: 5 and 20 (cowboy); © Felicia Martinez, 106 (cheese); © D. Young Wolf, 102 (totem pole)
Photo Researchers, Inc.: © David R. Frazier, 45 (t l)
The Picture Cube: 75 (b l); © Robb Helfrick, 74 (b r); © Dennis Macdonald, 78 (b r); © Lawrence Sawyer, 55 (b r)
© Paul Rezendes, 87 (b r)
© Eugene G. Schultz, 107 (b)
© South Dakota Tourism, 91 (b)
Tom Stack & Associates: © Tom Algire, 48 (t r); © Terry Donnelly, 83 (c l); © Mark Newman, 12 (t l)
The Stock Market: 11 (b l); © Bob Abraham, 30 (t l); © Richard Berenholtz, 72 (b l); © James Blank, 106 (t r); © Chromosohm/Joe Sohm, 51 (b l); © Anthony Edgeworth, 48 (b r); © Terry Eggers, 103 (b c); © Douglas Faulkner, 5 and 26 (manatee); © Jim Foster, 35 (t l); © Mark Gamba, 5 and 20 (skier); © Mark & Audrey Gibson, 100 (t r); © Bob Gomel, 94 (longhorn); © Ted Horowitz, 31 (t r); © Bob Krist, 89 (c l); © Thom Lang, 70 (chiles); © Harvey Lloyd, 86 (b l); © Don Mason, 12 (salmon); © Benjamin Mendlowitz, 50 (t r); © Lance Nelson, 85 (Hershey signs); © Kunio Owaki, 93 (b r); © Kim Robbie, 50 (b r); © Pete Saloutos, 70 (b r); © Ron Sanford, 10 (b r); © Savage, 101 (c r); © Alan Schein, 68 (b l); 70 (b r), 98 (t l) © Zefa
© Stock Montage, 35 (c l)
Tony Stone Images: 19 (b l); © James Balog, 21 (t l); © Ryan Beyer, 17 (b l); © Gary Brettnacher, 33 (b r); © Rosemary Calvert, 94 (t r), 95 (c); © Cosmo Condina, 73 (b l); © D.E. Cox, 53 (b r); © Robert E. Daemmrich, 94 (b r); © Doris De Witt, 42 (t r); © John Elk, 15 (t l), 28 (c l), 56 (t r); © Barbara Filet, 15 (b l); © Tim Flach, 14 (gila); © Charles Gupton, 89 (b r); © Chip Henderson, 20 (Mesa Verde); © Chris Honeywell, 44 (b l); © Hulton Getty, 89 (c); © George Hunter, 20 (b c); © H. Richard Johns, 102 (barn); © G. Brad Lewis, 30 (t r), 96 (t r); © Renee Lynn, 22 (leaf); © David Muench, 40 (b l), 64 (Lake Tahoe); © Matthew McVay, 91 (c r); © Vito Palmisano, 34 (b l); © Peter Pearson, 35 (b r); © Jim Pickerell, 25 (b c), 104 (b r); © Greg Probst, 14 (b r); © Jake Rais, 24 (b l); © Donovan Reese, 58 (b r); © Bill Ross, 92 (t r); © Andy Sacks, 11 (t l); © Joseph Sohm, 38 (t r); © Bob Thomason, 28 (b l); © Larry Ulrich, 14 (t r), 46 (t r), 82 (c r), 90 (t r), 104 (t r); © Terry Vine, 95 (c l); © Randy Wells, 74 (t r); © Rosemary Weller, 16 (c r); © Art Wolfe, 12 (b l), 26 (panther)
SuperStock International: 12 (b), 16 (rice), 18 (b r), 20 (sheep), 21 (b l), 24 (b r), 32 (b r), 33 (t l), 39 (b l), 40 (c l), 43 (b r), 46 (b r), 52 (t r and c r), 60 (b r), 62 (t r), 63 (Boys Town statue), 70 (t r), 80 (b c), 84 (t r), 108 (elk)
Travel Stock: © Ric Ergenbright, 85 (b r)
Unicorn Stock Photos: © Martha McBride, 42 (t l)
Virginia Tourism Corporation: © Nik Wheeler, 100 (t l)
Visuals Unlimited: 14 (tree frog, rattlesnake); © Jeff J. Daly, 52 (t l); © Mark E. Gibson, 16 (b r), 39 (c r); © Dick Keen, 46 (b r); © Lindhom, 12 (fur seal); © Steve McCutcheon, 102 (b r); © Joe McDonald, 12 (polar bear); © Glenn Oliver, 5 and 26 (alligator); © Kjell B. Sandved, 49 (b r); © Doug Sokell, 90 (t l); © Inga Spence, 102 (apples), 103 (c l); © Gilbert Twiest, 78 (t l)
© Peter Weimann, 107 (b r)
West Virginia Division of Tourism: © David Fattaleh, 104 (rafting on New River), 105 (b)
© Fred Whitehead, 48 (crab)
© Woodfin Camp & Associates, 103 (c r)
© Wyoming Division of Tourism, 109 (wagon train)

State emblems from *Young Students Learning Library*. Copyright © 1994 by Atlas Editions, Inc. All rights reserved. Used with permission.

RAND McNALLY

Children's Illustrated Atlas of the United States
Copyright © 2006 by Rand McNally & Company
randmcnally.com

Published and printed in the United States of America
Library of Congress Control Number: 2005922961

For information on licensing and copyright permissions, please contact us at licensing@randmcnally.com

ISBN: 528-93459-7
10 9 8 7 6 5 4 3 2

Contents

Life in the Year 1000

A thousand years ago, hundreds of thousands of people lived on the land that was to become the United States of America. Many distinct languages were spoken by these people, and hundreds of cultures flourished. The people were builders, explorers, farmers, hunters, and inventors. They built large, thriving communities. They created a network of footpaths and traded goods across the continent. Their ancestors began living here at least 12,000 years ago and perhaps as long as 35,000 years ago. Their descendants live here still. Modern-day Native Americans are now part of their own tribal communities and nations. They are also part of the country of the United States of America, which is not yet 250 years old.

① The Northwest Coast Peoples

Native Americans on the northwest coast enjoyed a life of abundance. They had rivers filled with salmon and the ocean filled with seals and many kinds of fish. The thick forests were home to deer and other game animals. And the gigantic trees were perfect for building houses and large sturdy canoes for water travel.

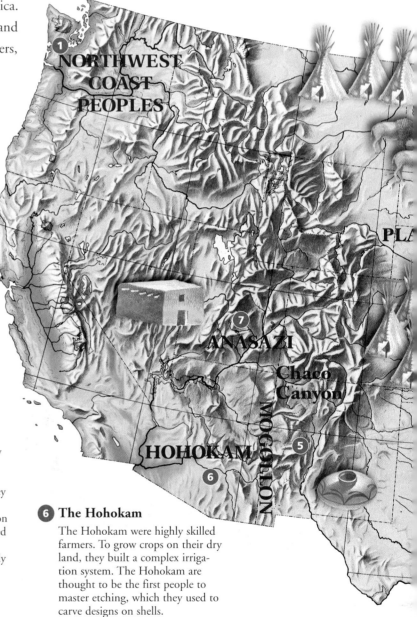

⑦ The Anasazi

The Anasazi developed a new form of architecture: above-ground stone and adobe dwellings called pueblos. They built the pueblos atop mesas and later along cliffs in canyon walls. The Anasazi also created elaborate painted pottery, turquoise jewelry, and brightly colored clothing.

⑥ The Hohokam

The Hohokam were highly skilled farmers. To grow crops on their dry land, they built a complex irrigation system. The Hohokam are thought to be the first people to master etching, which they used to carve designs on shells.

⑧ The Inuit

The Inuit lived in huts made from logs, whale ribs, stone, mud, and other available materials. They hunted fish, seals, sea lions, walruses, and whales, as well as land mammals, for food.

⑤ The Mogollon

The Mogollon people were farmers, house builders, and potters. They were also fine weavers of clothing, blankets, and baskets. The Mogollons' in-ground pit houses protected them from the temperature extremes of the region.

2 The Plains Indians

The Plains Indians were seminomadic, traveling much of the year but staying in one place the rest of the year. Millions of buffalo roamed the plains in the year 1000, and the Plains Indians followed the herds. They depended on buffalo as their main source of food, clothing, and tools. They hunted on foot using bows and arrows, and lived in tepees made of animal skins.

3 The Northern Iroquoian

The Northern Iroquoian were hunters, farmers, and traders. They lived in villages of bark-covered longhouses of varying sizes. Some of the longhouses were so large that they housed as many as 20 families.

Norsemen

Sailors led by Leif Ericsson explored areas along the eastern coast of what was to become North America.

NORTHERN IROQUOIAN

DIANS

Cahokia

MISSISSIPPIANS

4 The Mississippians

The Mississippians were master farmers. They lived mostly in river valleys, where the soil was rich. They also had an extensive trade network among themselves and other Native American groups. The Mississippians used materials from various regions to make tools and jewelry. They built huge burial and temple mounds. Cahokia, the largest collection of these mounds, held nearly 100 burial and temple mounds and a population of thousands.

N
W   E
S

Trade

By A.D. 1000, the continent was connected by trade routes. Mississippians had a strong trade network, which connected them to other Native American groups.

Travel by Land	Travel by Water
A network of footpaths wound across the continent, allowing Native Americans to travel from region to region for trade and other purposes.	Native Americans also traveled on rivers and lakes in dugouts and canoes.

What was traded?	Where did the goods come from?
pottery, woven goods, copper	Great Lakes area
obsidian	present-day Wyoming
mica	Appalachian Mountains
gold and silver	present-day Canada
conch shells	Gulf of Mexico

CANADA

WASHINGTON
Olympia ● Seattle
Columbia
Mt. Rainier
14,410 Ft.
4,392 M.
Mt. St. Helens
8,364 Ft.
2,549 M.
Portland ● Mt. Hood
11,239 Ft.
3,426 M.
Salem ★
Columbia

CASCADE RANGE

OREGON

Goose
Lake

Shasta
Lake

PACIFIC
OCEAN

Pyramid
Lake

Sacramento

Sacramento ★
CALIFORNIA
San Francisco ●
● Oakland
● San Jose
Carson City ●
Lake Tahoe
NEVADA

SIERRA NEVADA

Boundary Peak
13,140 Ft.
4,005 M.

Mt. Whitney
14,494 Ft.
4,418 M.

San Joaquin

COAST RANGES

Los Angeles ●
● Long Beach

San Diego ●

Salton
Sea

MONTANA
Helena ●

Flathead
Lake

Clark Fork

BITTERROOT RANGE

SALMON RIVER
MOUNTAINS

Salmon

Boise ●
IDAHO
Borah Peak
12,662 Ft.
3,859 M.

Snake

Snake

American
Falls Res.

GREAT
BASIN

Humboldt

Great
Salt
Lake

Salt Lake City ●

WASATCH RA.

UTAH

Lake
Powell

Las Vegas ●
Lake Mead

Colorado

ARIZONA

Humphreys Peak
12,633 Ft.
3,851 M.

Phoenix ★

Gila

Milk

Missouri

Billings ●
Granite Peak
12,799 Ft.
3,901 M.

Yellowstone

Yellowstone
Lake

Gannett Pk.
13,804 Ft.
4,207 M.

WYOMING

Flaming
Gorge Res.

Green

MOUNTAINS

Kings Peak
13,528 Ft.
4,123 M.

Colorado

Cheyenne ●

COLORADO
Mt. Elbert
14,433 Ft.
4,399 M.

● Denver
● Colorado Springs

Rio Grande

+ Wheeler Peak
13,161 Ft.
4,011 M.

Santa Fe ●

● Albuquerque

NEW MEXICO

Little Colorado

Salt

BLACK RA.

SACRAMENTO MTS.

El Paso ●
+ Guadalupe Peak
8,749 Ft.
2,667 M.

Rio Grande

Tucson ●

Tongue

Powder

NORTH DAKOTA
Bismarck ★

Sheyenne

Souris

Moreau

BADLANDS

Cheyenne
BLACK HILLS Harney Peak
7,242 Ft.
2,207 M.

Lake
Oahe

SOUTH DAKOTA
★ Pierre

White

Lake Francis
Case

Niobrara

North Loup

NEBRASKA

North Platte

South Platte

Platte

Republican

KANSAS

Smoky Hill

Arkansas

OKLA

Amarillo ●
Oklahoma Ci

Canadian

Red

TEXAS

Cimarron

Pecos

Fort Wo

San Antonio ●

Nueces

Rio Grande

M E X I C O

RUS.

Yukon

ALASKA
Mt. McKinley
20,320 Ft.
6,194 M.

CANADA

● Anchorage

Juneau ★

PACIFIC
OCEAN

Scale 1:29,000,000; One inch to 457 miles.

Honolulu ★

PACIFIC
OCEAN

HAWAII

Mauna Kea
13,796 Ft.
4,205 M.

Scale 1:12,500,000; One inch to 197 miles.

STATES

GULF OF MEXICO

Map Legend

⊛ Washington, D.C.   **National capital**

★ Jefferson City   **State capital**

● New York   **Population 1,000,000 or more**

• Las Vegas   **Population 250,000-1,000,000**

〰 Lake Texoma   **Lake**

〰 Platte   **River**

0	100	200	300	400 Miles	
0	100	200	300	400	500	600 Kilometers

Scale 1:12,000,000; One inch to 189 miles.

© Rand McNally
N-CUS24000-P1- -1-1-2

United States Facts

United States Flag

Capital
Washington, D.C.

Area
3,537,438 square miles
(9,161,929 sq km)

Population
293,655,404

Principal Rivers
Mississippi River,
Missouri River,
Rio Grande,
Yukon River,
Arkansas River,
Colorado River,
Red River,
Columbia River,
Snake River,
Ohio River

Highest Point
Mount McKinley,
20,320 feet (6,194 m)

ALABAMA

Alabama's name comes from a Native American tribe that once lived in the area, the Alibamu. *Alibamu* means "clearer of thickets." Alabama is in the Deep South, and when people think of this state they may think of southern hospitality, huge houses with broad front porches, or even peanuts. Alabama does have all of these things. It also has beautiful coastal areas, an abundance of forests, and vast mineral resources.

An elegant mansion in Eufaula dating from the pre-Civil War era

Water hyacinths

Geography and Climate

Alabama has a hot, wet climate that is sometimes cooled by breezes off the Gulf of Mexico. The northern part of the state is full of pine forests, hills, and many lakes and rivers. In the southern part of the state are swamps, beaches, and bayous (shallow channels with slow-moving water). Alabama has more than 1,350 miles (2,160 kilometers) of waterways. Not only are these lakes and rivers beautiful, they also provide a convenient way to transport goods in and out of the state.

Cotton and Peanuts

In the early 1900s, an insect called the boll weevil destroyed much of the cotton crop in Alabama, causing economic disaster for the state. Farmers had already begun rotating their crops — that is, growing different crops from year to year — to help keep the soil fertile. The boll weevil attack made the farmers increase their planting of peanuts and soybeans. The scientist George Washington Carver came up with more than 300 uses for peanuts. His discoveries greatly helped Alabama's economy. At Tuskegee University, there is a museum devoted to Carver's achievements.

Bobcats roam the Appalachian Mountains in northern Alabama. Some other Alabama animals are deer and wild turkeys.

Mobile, Alabama's only seaport, is one of the busiest in the country.

Timeline

1519
Alonso Álvarez de Piñeda arrives in Mobile Bay

1540
Hernando DeSoto claims the land for Spain

1763
France cedes territory to Great Britain

1814
Andrew Jackson defeats Creek Indians in Battle of Horseshoe Bend

1819
Alabama becomes 22nd state

1832
Railroad operation begins

1854
Public schools established statewide

1861
Constitution of Confederacy drawn up in Montgomery

1881
Booker T. Washington establishes Tuskegee Normal and Industrial Institute

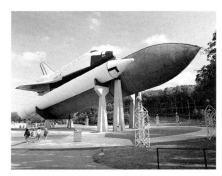

An outdoor model of the space shuttle in Huntsville

3-2-1, Blast Off!

The U.S. Space & Rocket Center in Huntsville is the world's largest space museum. The museum is home to more missiles than any other site in the world, and there are more than 60 hands-on exhibits for visitors to explore. NASA's George C. Marshall Space Flight Center is also in Huntsville. The booster rockets for the Apollo II spacecraft were made at this center. The rockets carried the spacecraft all the way to the moon in 1969.

The World War II battleship U.S.S. Alabama, in Mobile

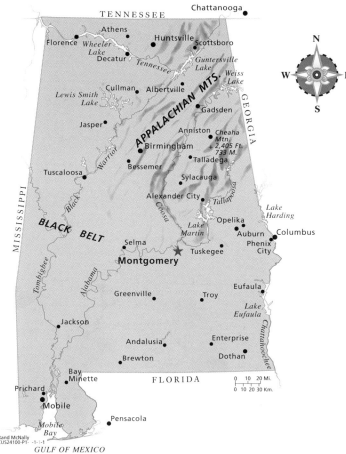

© Rand McNally
N-CUS24100-P1- -1-1-1

GULF OF MEXICO

Rosa Parks at the front of the bus, December 21, 1956.

The Way It Was . . . Rosa Parks and the Bus Boycott

A landmark event of the civil rights movement took place in Montgomery in 1955. On December 1 of that year, Rosa Parks was taking a bus home from work. Parks was sitting in the "blacks only" section of the bus, but she knew that if more white people came aboard she would be expected to give up her seat to them. Parks was tired, though, and as the bus became more crowded, she refused to stand up. For her action, she was taken off the bus, arrested, and led to jail. When word of the incident spread, African Americans in Montgomery began a boycott against the bus company. The boycott, which lasted more than a year, eventually forced integration of the buses.

1909
Wright Brothers start
first flight school

1960
NASA opens George C. Marshall
Space Flight Center

1970
U.S. Space & Rocket
Center opens to public

1993
Gov. Guy Hunt removed from office
after conviction for misuse of funds

1933
Tennessee Valley
Authority created

1962
Gov. George C.
Wallace elected to
the first of four terms

1965
Martin Luther King, Jr.'s
march leads to passage of
Voting Right Acts of 1965

2005
Condoleezza Rice is first
African American woman to
serve as U.S. Secretary of State

ALASKA

The name *Alaska* comes from a Native American word that means "great land" — a perfect description of this amazing place. By far the largest of the fifty states, Alaska covers more than twice as much area as Texas, the second largest state. Alaska stretches north of the

Igloo and snowshoes

Arctic Circle, and parts of the state lie only a few miles from Russia. Of the 20 highest mountain peaks in the United States, 17 are in Alaska. That includes the highest mountain in North America — towering Mount McKinley in Denali National Park.

Seward's Folly?

Many Americans were shocked when United States Secretary of State William H. Seward bought Alaska from Russia in 1867. They called Alaska names like Seward's Folly and Seward's Icebox. It's true that Alaska has thousands of glaciers and large areas of frozen plain called tundra. Alaska, however, is hardly a frozen wasteland. Summers in the interior can be hot. With 20 hours of sunshine on summer days, fruits and vegetables grow to two or three times their normal size. Alaska also has an abundance of natural resources, such as gold and oil.

The Iditarod Trail Sled Dog Race is run every March from Anchorage to Nome, a distance of more than 1,000 miles (1,609 km).

The St. Elias Mountains rise along the icy waters of the Gulf of Alaska.

Wild Animals

- **Polar bears** live along the coast of the Arctic Ocean. Alaska is the only state with polar bears.

- **Fur seals**  arrive at Alaska's Pribilof Islands each spring. Seal pups are born and spend their first summer there before the herd swims south for winter.

- **Moose, caribou, elk,** and **reindeer** roam Alaska. In fact, the largest moose in the world are those that live in Alaska.

Timeline

1784
First Russian settlement in Alaska

1878
Salmon canneries established

1884
Alaska's first public schools established

1741
Vitus Bering lands on Kayak Island, Alaska

1867
U.S. buys Alaska from Russia for $7,200,000

1880
Joe Juneau discovers gold

1912
Alaska becomes a territory

Alaska Flag

Willow Ptarmigan

Forget-me-not

Sitka Spruce

Nickname
The Last Frontier

Capital
Juneau

Area
571,951 square miles
(1,481,347 sq km)
Rank: 1st

Population
655,400
Rank: 47th

Statehood
January 3, 1959
49th state admitted

Principal River
Yukon River

Highest Point
Mount McKinley,
20,320 feet (6,194 m)

Motto
North to the future

Song
"Alaska's Flag"

Famous People
Tom Bodett,
Susan Butcher,
Libby Riddles,
Jefferson "Soapy" Smith

People and Places

Alaska Natives make up about 14 percent of the state's population. Alaska Natives include Eskimos, Aleuts, and American Indians. Despite its enormous size, Alaska has a small population. Most of the state has fewer than two people per square mile. The bulk of the population lives in Fairbanks, Anchorage, Juneau, and other cities along the southeast coast. Juneau, the state capital, is surrounded by mountains and water and can be reached only by airplane or boat. There are no roads leading to it.

The Way It Was . . .
The Great Race of Mercy

Alaska was still a frontier territory in the mid-1920s. Dogsledding was often the only way to get from one settlement to another in winter. In January 1925, the town of Nome was hit by an outbreak of diphtheria. Without the right medicine, the outbreak would become deadly. The nearest supply of medicine was in Anchorage. It could be sent by rail only as far as Nenana, hundreds of miles from Nome. And so the "great race of mercy" began. Twenty dogsled drivers, or mushers, and their dog teams carried the precious medicine from Nenana to Nome in relays. Amazingly, the teams completed their mission in fewer than six days. They were hailed as heroes.

Gunnar Kasson, musher of the last relay team, holds Balto, the lead dog.

1942
Japan invades
Aleutian Islands

1942
Alaska Highway
completed

1957
Oil discovered on
Kenai Peninsula

1959
Alaska becomes
49th state

1964
Good Friday
earthquake

1968
Oil discovered near
Prudhoe Bay

1977
Pipeline completed
from Prudhoe Bay
to Valdez

1989
Exxon Valdez spills 11 million gallons of
crude oil in Prince William Sound

1992
Mt. Spurr eruptions
deposit volcanic
ash on Anchorage

2002
Major earthquake
along the Denali Fault

ARIZONA

The name *Arizona* comes from a Native American word that means "place of small springs." Water is indeed precious in this dry state. There is more to Arizona than sunny skies and lack of rain, however. Arizona is a land of spectacular contrasts, where hot, dry, nearly barren desert is only hours away from forests and snow-capped mountains. In addition to its beautiful landscapes, Arizona is home to many rare plants and animals.

The White House Ruins lie in the shelter of towering rock walls in Canyon de Chelly National Monument.

Natural Wonders

From corner to corner and every place in between, Arizona's landscape is breathtaking. The Painted Desert has hills and terraces of yellow, red, pink, blue, and tan rock. Ancient tree trunks have turned to rainbow-colored stone in Petrified Forest National Park. Towering cacti at Saguaro National Monument sprout graceful arms along their prickly trunks. The most famous natural wonder in the state, the Grand Canyon, displays dozens of colorful rock layers, some of which are two billion years old.

Arizona Wildlife

- **Gila monsters** are one of only two kinds of poisonous lizards in the world.

- **Arizona tree frogs** live in the forests. These tiny two-inch-long (five-centimeter-long) amphibians have multi-colored skin that helps them hide from predators.

- **Ridge-nosed rattlesnakes** are less than 24 inches (61 centimeters) long.

The majestic Grand Canyon measures 277 miles (443 km) long, 18 miles (29 km) wide, and more than a mile (1.6 km) deep.

The Mission San Xavier del Bac near Tucson is a stately presence against the Arizona sky.

Timeline

1200
Hopi village of Oraibi founded

1540
Grand Canyon first seen by Spanish explorers

1821
Arizona becomes part of Mexico

1848
Most of Arizona becomes part of U.S.

1853
Remainder of Arizona becomes part of U.S.

1881
Gunfight at the O.K. Corr[al] Tombstone on October 26

1886
Apache lead[er] Geronimo surrenders

The Navajo of Arizona once lived in dwellings called hogans.

People and Places

Arizona is home to many Native American people. Indian reservations (more than 20 of them) cover almost one-fourth of the state's land. Yet the reservations, as well as most of the rest of Arizona, are thinly populated. In fact, 85 percent of the population resides on just two percent of the land. Arizona's major urban centers, Phoenix and Tucson, have been growing steadily since the early 1950s, when air conditioning made living and working in the desert climate comfortable year-round.

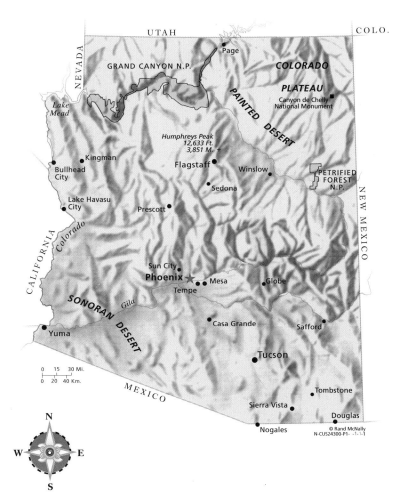

Boot Hill, the resting place of some infamous Old West gunslingers, is a popular tourist attraction in Tombstone.

The Way It Was . . . The Last of the Old West

Arizona remained part of the "lawless Old West" longer than any other place. One reason was the rugged terrain. It was easy for outlaws to disappear in the Arizona mountains and canyons. Also, for a long time, outlaws could avoid capture by fleeing to neighboring Mexico or even just to the next county. It was not until 1901, when the Arizona Rangers were organized, that non-federal lawmen were allowed to pursue criminals across county lines. By then, Arizona citizens were calling for statehood, but politicians in Washington, D.C. felt that Arizona was unfit. Arizona finally became a state in 1912, the last of the 48 contiguous states to be admitted.

Wyatt Earp was marshal in the raucous town of Tombstone.

State Facts

Arizona Flag

Cactus Wren

Saguaro Cactus Blossom

Palo Verde

Nickname
Grand Canyon State

Capital
Phoenix

Area
113,635 square miles
(294,314 sq km)
Rank: 6th

Population
5,743,800
Rank: 18th

Statehood
February 14, 1912
48th state admitted

Principal Rivers
Colorado River,
Gila River

Highest Point
Humphreys Peak,
12,633 feet (3,851 m)

Motto
Ditat Deus
(God enriches)

Song
"Arizona March Song"
and "Arizona"

Famous People
Cochise, Geronimo,
Barry M. Goldwater,
Sandra Day O'Connor

1911
Roosevelt Dam completed

1919
Grand Canyon National Park founded

1964
Senator Barry M. Goldwater runs for president

1993
Central Arizona Project diverts water from Colorado River to Tucson

1912
Arizona becomes 48th state

1930
Clyde Tombaugh discovers the planet Pluto at Lowell Observatory in Flagstaff

1981
Justice Sandra Day O'Connor becomes first woman on U.S. Supreme Court

2004
One of the world's largest telescopes dedicated at Mt. Graham

ARKANSAS

The scenic Buffalo River is popular with canoeists and nature-lovers.

Arkansas comes from a Native American word that means "downstream people." The state's eastern border is formed by the Mississippi River as it flows south toward the Gulf of Mexico. The land of Arkansas falls into two distinct regions: the highlands in the west and north and the lowlands in the east and south. Arkansas has plenty of fertile farmland and a variety of natural resources, including coal, natural gas, oil, and bauxite, which is used to make aluminum.

Digging for Diamonds

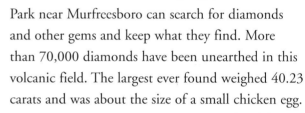

Arkansas is home to the only public diamond field in North America. Visitors to Crater of Diamonds State Park near Murfreesboro can search for diamonds and other gems and keep what they find. More than 70,000 diamonds have been unearthed in this volcanic field. The largest ever found weighed 40.23 carats and was about the size of a small chicken egg.

Rice Fields

Because rice grows best when its roots are underwater, the low, wet areas of Arkansas along the Mississippi River are perfect for rice farming. Arkansas produces more rice than any other state. Some farmers have converted their fields and have begun growing crops other than rice, such as soybeans and cotton. Some others have flooded their rice fields to use them as fish hatcheries.

Rice plants

Panning for diamonds in Crater of Diamonds State Park

Timeline

1541
Hernando De Soto arrives in Arkansas

1673
Jacques Marquette and Louis Jolliet explore area

1682
René-Robert Cavelier, Sieur de La Salle, visits area

1686
Henri de Tonti establishes settlement at Arkansas Post

1763
France cedes area to Spain

1800
Spain returns Arkansas to France

1803
U.S. acquires Arkansas as part of Louisiana Purchase

1819
Arkansas becomes a territory

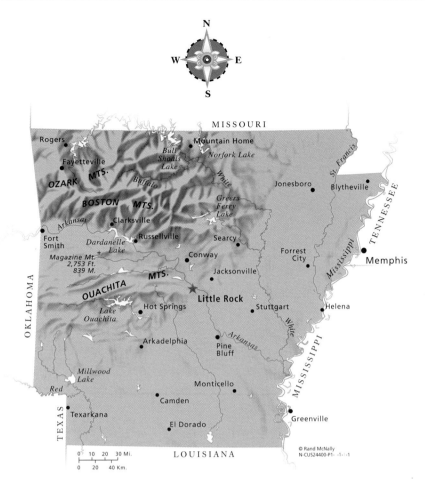

Built in 1889, the Pulaski County Courthouse is a landmark in Little Rock, the state capital.

Cold and Hot Springs

Imagine millions of gallons of cold water bubbling out of the earth each hour. This is what happens every day at Mammoth Spring in the Ozark Mountains of Arkansas. The state has many natural springs. Some springs gush hot water, which is good for soaking. Eureka Springs has more than 65 springs, and Hot Springs consists of 47 hot springs. Many vacationers visit the resort towns that have grown up at Eureka Springs and Hot Springs.

Bathhouse Row in Hot Springs National Park preserves an atmosphere of leisure.

Jim Bowie

The Way It Was . . .
An Arkansas Toothpick

What is an Arkansas toothpick? Believe it or not, it's a famous knife. James Black moved into the Arkansas territory in 1824 and became known as a maker of excellent knives. The frontiersman Jim Bowie heard about Black's knives and decided that he had to have one. Black designed a special knife for Bowie. Soon other people wanted the same style of knife, which became known as a Bowie knife. Black intended to pass along his knife-making secrets, but he died before he was able to share what he knew. Bowie hunting knives were very useful. People used them to skin deer, slit fish, and cut chunks of bear meat. They even used the sharp points of the knives to pick their teeth. That is how the Bowie knife got the nickname "Arkansas toothpick."

State Facts

Arkansas Flag

Mockingbird

Apple Blossom

Pine

Nickname
The Natural State

Capital
Little Rock

Area
52,068 square miles
(134,856 sq km)
Rank: 32nd

Population
2,752,600
Rank: 32nd

Statehood
June 15, 1836
25th state admitted

Principal Rivers
Arkansas River,
Mississippi River,
White River

Highest Point
Magazine Mountain,
2,753 feet (839 m)

Motto
Regnat populus
(The people rule)

Song
"Arkansas"

Famous People
Maya Angelou,
William Jefferson Clinton,
Douglas MacArthur

1836
Arkansas becomes
25th state

1906
Diamonds discovered
in Pike County

1957
National Guard called into Little Rock
high school to enforce integration

2004
Governor Mike Huckabee launches
Healthy Arkansas Initiative

1821
Capital moves from
Arkansas Post to
Little Rock

1861
Arkansas joins the
Confederacy

1921
First auto, gas, and oil
taxes levied to finance
roads and highways

1962
First Wal-Mart
store opens in
Rogers

1992
Arkansas governor William
Jefferson Clinton elected
42nd U.S. President

CALIFORNIA

Spanish explorers of the 1500s named California after a treasure island in a popular tale of the time. Although not an island, California has many treasures. The greatest gold rush in history began after the shiny metal was discovered in California in 1848. Since then, California's abundant sunshine and other appealing

features have continued to attract tourists and people who want to make a fresh start. As a result, California has more people than any other state and one of the most diverse populations in the world.

Natural Diversity

California's natural diversity is as amazing as its diverse population. The state's mountainous areas include the low, forested Coast Ranges and the towering granite peaks of the Sierra Nevada. Between those lies the Central Valley, one of the world's most productive farming regions. In contrast, much of southeastern California is a desert. This wide variety of habitats gives California more types of plants and animals than any other state.

Rugged mountains along California's central coast plunge into the blue waters of the Pacific Ocean.

An Economic Powerhouse

California ranks first among the states in manufacturing and agriculture. High-tech industries are especially important, producing computer, communication, and medical equipment. California also leads all states in the production of milk, eggs, tomatoes, lettuce, almonds, strawberries, and other agricultural products. Most American wine comes from grapes grown in California. The entertainment industry is a vital part of California's economy, too. Hollywood was a sleepy Los Angeles suburb when the first movie studio was built there in 1911. Hollywood is now the world's movie and television capital.

This famous sign sits high on a hillside overlooking Hollywood.

Orange grove in California's fertile San Joaquin Valley

Timeline

1542 Juan Rodriguez Cabrillo explores San Diego Bay

1579 Francis Drake claims land for England

1697 First mission established

1781 Los Angeles is founded

1822 California becomes part of Mexico

1841 First wagon train reaches California

1846 U.S. takes control during Mexican War

1847 California becomes a U.S. territory

1849 Gold rush begins; prospectors nick-named "Forty-Nin

San Francisco's Golden Gate Bridge

Two Man-Made Wonders

Golden Gate Bridge is one of the world's largest suspension bridges. Spanning the entrance to San Francisco Bay, the massive but delicate-looking structure is a spectacular sight. Another phenomenal structure is the Hearst Castle, located north of San Luis Obisipo. It was the estate of newspaper publisher William Randolph Hearst. Visitors can tour the mansion, which contains priceless art and antiques.

Hearst Castle sits atop the "Enchanted Hill." The estate took 28 years to build.

OREGON

REDWOOD NAT'L. PK.
Yreka
Goose Lake
Alturas
Eureka
Lake Shasta
Redding
LASSEN VOLCANIC NAT'L. PK.
Sacramento
Chico
Reno
Ukiah
Yuba City
Lake Tahoe
Santa Rosa
COAST RANGES
SIERRA
Sacramento
Berkeley
YOSEMITE NAT'L. PK.
NEVADA
Mono Lake
San Francisco
Oakland
Stockton
NEVADA
San Jose
Modesto
San Joaquin
Santa Cruz
Merced
KINGS CANYON N.P.
Monterey Bay
Fresno
Mt. Whitney 14,494 Ft. 4,418 M.
Monterey
Salinas
Visalia
SEQUOIA NAT'L. PK.
DEATH VALLEY N.P.
Las Vegas
PACIFIC OCEAN
San Luis Obispo
Bakersfield
Barstow
MOJAVE DESERT
Needles
SAN RAFAEL MTS.
Lancaster
Santa Barbara
Oxnard
Pasadena
San Bernardino
JOSHUA TREE NAT'L. PK.
SAN MIGUEL ISLAND
Los Angeles
Riverside
ARIZONA
SANTA ROSA ISLAND
SANTA CRUZ ISLAND
Long Beach
Anaheim
Palm Springs
Blythe
CHANNEL ISLANDS NATIONAL PARK
SANTA CATALINA ISLAND
Oceanside
Salton Sea
SAN NICOLAS ISLAND
San Diego
El Centro
Colorado
SAN CLEMENTE ISLAND
Tijuana
MEXICO

0 10 20 30 Mi.
0 20 40 Km.
© Rand McNally
N-CUS24500-P1- -1- -1 -1

N W E S

Junípero Serra (1713-1784)

The Way It Was . . . El Camino Real

In 1769, a Spanish expedition was sent north from Mexico to take control of California. A gentle, frail Roman Catholic priest named Junípero Serra accompanied the soldiers. After a grueling 800-mile (1,287-kilometer) walk, the expedition reached San Diego Bay. There they built Mission San Diego de Alcalá, the first in a chain of 21 missions that would be erected along California's coast. The missions were deliberately spaced about one day's walk apart. The trail between them became known as *El Camino Real* (The Royal Road). Today Serra's statue stands in Statuary Hall in the United States Capitol.

State Facts

California Flag

California Valley Quail

Golden Poppy

California Redwood

Nickname
The Golden State

Capital
Sacramento

Area
155,959 miles
(403,932 sq km)
Rank: 3rd

Population
35,893,800
Rank: 1st

Statehood
September 9, 1850
31st state admitted

Principal Rivers
Colorado River,
Sacramento River,
San Joaquin River

Highest Point
Mount Whitney,
14,494 feet (4,418 m)

Motto
Eureka (I have found it)

Song
"I Love You, California"

Famous People
Ansel Adams,
Jack London,
Marilyn Monroe,
Richard Nixon,
Sally Ride,
John Steinbeck

1911
First Hollywood movie studio established

1977
Apple Computer founded

1989
Earthquake shakes San Francisco Bay area

2002
Lakers win third consecutive NBA championship

1850
California becomes 31st state

1937
Golden Gate Bridge opens

1955
Disneyland welcomes first visitors

1984
Los Angeles hosts Olympic Games

1994
Earthquake hits Los Angeles

COLORADO

The majestic Rocky Mountains form a bumpy backbone through the center of Colorado and give it a higher average elevation than any other state. The thick, powdery snow that covers the Rockies in winter makes the state a skier's paradise. East of the Rockies stretch the Great Plains, and west lies an area of plateaus, hills, and valleys. *Colorado* is a Spanish word meaning "colored red." The name was first given to the Colorado River, which flows through red sandstone canyons.

Colorado Attractions

Millions of visitors flock to Colorado each year. Colorado's many attractions include Rocky Mountain and Mesa Verde National Parks and Great Sand Dunes National Monument. Rocky Mountain National Park has magnificent scenery, including more than 100 peaks higher than 11,000 feet (3,350 meters). The park's abundant wildlife and plant life include bighorn sheep and hundreds of flowering plants, some of which take years to grow at high altitude. Mesa Verde National Park features cliff dwellings built by the Anasazi before A.D. 1300. Cliff Palace, the largest of these dwellings, has more than 200 rooms. Great Sand Dunes National Monument features the largest dunes in North America, some as high as 700 feet (212 meters).

Of the 80 mountain peaks in the United States that rise above 14,000 feet (4,200 m), 54 are located in Colorado.

Using sandstone blocks and mud mortar, the Anasazi built complex dwellings.

Making a Living

- **Mining,** including oil, natural gas, and coal, is a major source of income.

- **Ranching** is a tradition in Colorado.

- **Skiing** is big business in places such as Aspen, Vail, Telluride, and Steamboat Springs.

Timeline

1540 Francisco Vásquez de Coronado is first European to explore area

1706 Juan de Ulibassi claims region for Spain

1803 Northeastern Colorado joins U.S. as part of Louisiana Purchase

1806 Zebulon Pike spots Pikes Peak

1833 First white settlement, Bent's Fort, is built

1848 Western Colorado becomes part of U.S. after end of Mexican war

1858 Gold discovered in Cherry Creek

1861 Colorado becomes a territory

1870 Railroads connect Colorado to eastern U.S.

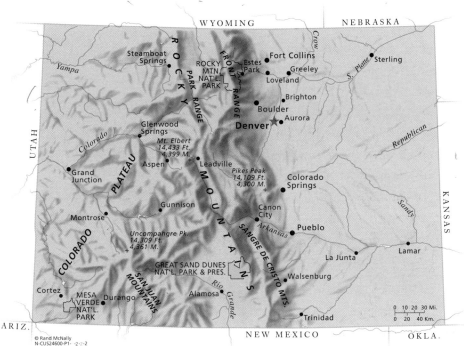

The Rocky Mountains form a spectacular backdrop for the Denver skyline.

The Capital City

Denver, like most of Colorado's major cities, grew up where the Great Plains meet the Rocky Mountains. Denver was founded in 1858, after the discovery of gold along Cherry Creek. The discovery drew thousands of gold seekers. Appropriately, modern Denver is the site of a United States mint. Besides storing part of the government's gold supply, the Denver mint makes millions of pennies and other coins each day.

Vermilion Peak rises over a stand of aspen trees.

From the Garden of the Gods, near Colorado Springs, Pikes Peak is visible in the distance.

The Way It Was . . . The Grand Peak

In 1806, United States Army general and explorer Zebulon Pike was ordered to explore a part of the Louisiana Purchase in what is now central Colorado. Pike's group spotted a mountain that Pike called the Grand Peak. Native Americans had known about the peak for a long time. Pike's attempt to climb the mountain failed, but he later published a popular book that described the Grand Peak in all its glory. In 1820, explorer Stephen Long became the first recorded person to reach the top of the Grand Peak, which is now called Pikes Peak. Today sightseers can reach the summit of Pikes Peak by trail, road, or railway.

1876
Colorado becomes
38th state

1929
Mammoth Bridge across
Royal Gorge opens

1959
Colorado-Big Thompson
Dam Project completed

1999
Columbine High
School shooting

2000
Census shows 30%
population increase

1906
Coin production begins
at U.S. Mint in Denver

1958
Air Force Academy opens
near Colorado Springs

1998, 1999
Denver Broncos win the
Super Bowl two years in a row

CONNECTICUT

Mystic Seaport is a re-creation of a 19th-century fishing village.

This stone wall is a typical feature of older Connecticut farms.

Stone-Walled Farms

Colonists cleared Connecticut's rocky soil so they could build homes and plant crops. The colonists used the dug-up rocks to build stone walls around their fields. The walls still serve as borders and are an interesting and appealing addition to the landscape of the state.

The name *Connecticut* comes from an Algonquian Indian word that means "beside the long tidal river." That river is the Connecticut River, which is the longest waterway in New England. It is about 410 miles (660 kilometers) long and flows southward through the center of the state. Connecticut has many historic sites and plenty of New England charm, with stone-walled farms, mill towns, seaports, and rolling, forested hills.

Industry and Forests

Connecticut is home to service industries such as insurance, real estate, and retail trade. The state also has a long history of manufacturing. Clocks, helicopters, submarines, computers, and aircraft parts are just a few of the many items that are made in Connecticut. Most industry in the state is centered in the larger cities. Much of the rest of the state — 60 percent of it, in fact — is covered with forests. That's more than any other New England state. There are nearly 100 forest preserves in Connecticut, and people come from miles around to admire the magnificent trees in autumn, when the leaves turn brilliant colors.

Connecticut's forests contain many maple, beech, birch, and hemlock trees. These trees produce the spectacular fall colors for which New England is known.

Timeline

1614
Area explored by Adriaen Block

1634
Settlements established along Connecticut River

1637
Pequot defeated by English settlers

1701
Yale University founded in New Haven

1764
The Hartford Courant, longest-published U.S. newspaper, established

1784
First American law school opens in Litchfield

1787
Connecticut Compromise adopted by Constitutional Convention

1788
Connecticut becomes 5th sta

N

MASSACHUSETTS

+ Mount Frissell
2,380 Ft.
725 M.

Barkhamsted Res.

Enfield

Windsor Locks

NEW YORK

Farmington

Torrington

West Hartford

Vernon

Manchester

Mansfield Hollow Lake

Putnam

RHODE ISLAND

★ Hartford

Bristol

New Britain

Willimantic

Quinebaug

Waterbury

Middletown

Meriden

Shetucket

Lake Candlewood

Norwich

Danbury

Housatonic

Quinnipiac

Connecticut

Thames

New London

Mystic

Saugatuck

Shelton

New Haven

© Rand McNally
N-CUS24700-P1- -1-1-1

Bridgeport

Fairfield

Norwalk

Greenwich

Stamford

Long Island Sound

0   10 Mi.
0   10 Km.

A State of Firsts

From the country's first law school — founded in Litchfield in 1784 — to the first use of anesthesia (by Dr. Horace Wells in 1844), Connecticut is a state of firsts. The United States insurance industry began in Hartford, which is still the insurance capital of the nation. In New Haven, Noah Webster published the first dictionary of American English in 1806. Connecticut was also home to the first tax-supported library and the first art museum open to the public.

The Way It Was . . . The Charter Oak

In 1639, Connecticut colonists created a document called the Fundamental Orders, which stated that a ruler should not be forced upon them. They petitioned England's King Charles for a charter that would make the colony nearly independent of the English governor stationed there. The king granted the request and sent the colonists a charter. In 1687, the charter was revoked. The English governor wanted to find the document and destroy it. According to legend, the colonists hid the charter in a hollow oak tree. The hollow tree became known as the Charter Oak. It stood as a proud reminder of Connecticut's principles until the 1800s, when a fierce storm knocked it over.

A colonist prepares to hide the charter from the King's agent.

1806
First American English dictionary published by Noah Webster

1875
Hartford becomes state capital

1984
Ellen Ash Peters becomes first woman named to Connecticut Supreme Court

1837
Railroad service begins

1974
Ella T. Grasso is first woman elected governor of a U.S. state without succeeding a husband

1990s
Native American casinos fuel economic growth

DELAWARE

Delaware, the second-smallest state in the United States, is 96 miles (154 kilometers) long and only nine miles (14 kilometers) wide at its narrowest point. This eastern state was one of the original 13 colonies and in 1787 became the first state to join the Union.

Delaware Bay got its name long before the state did. The bay was named for the first governor of Virginia, Lord De La Warr, even though De La Warr himself never set foot in Delaware.

Geography

Averaging about 60 feet (18 meters) above sea level, Delaware is the second lowest state in the United States–only Florida has a lower average elevation. Most of Delaware is flat, though the northern section features rolling foothills of the Appalachian Mountains. Forests cover one-third of the state, while sandy dunes line the coast. The Great Walking Dune of Cape Henlopen State Park moves a few feet every year. The winds along the coast cause the sand to shift, which makes the dune appear to move.

Snow geese, ducks, herons, egrets, and other waterfowl can be found in Bombay Hook National Wildlife Refuge.

Agriculture plays a major role in Delaware's economy.

Economy

Agriculture, fishing, manufacturing, and tourism are all important to Delaware's economy. Delaware is known for raising broiler chickens, which are used for their meat instead of their eggs. The state produces more than 225 million of them a year. Due to favorable corporate tax laws in Delaware, many companies are legally based, or incorporated, there.

Broiler chicken farm

Timeline

1631
Zwaanendael settlement established at Lewes

1638
Fort Christina founded

1664
Delaware becomes an English colony

1785
Delaware Gazette first published

1787
Delaware becomes first state

#1

1802
Du Pont Company founded

1832
Delaware Canal completed

1834
University of Delaware established

1897
State constitution adopted

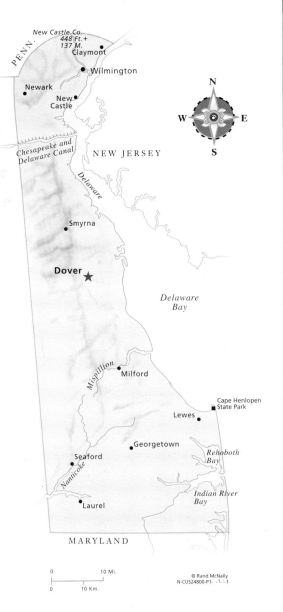

New Castle Co.
448 Ft.+
137 M.
PENN.
Claymont
Wilmington
Newark
New Castle
Chesapeake and
Delaware Canal
NEW JERSEY
Delaware
Smyrna
Dover ★
Delaware
Bay
Mispillion
Milford
Cape Henlopen
State Park
Lewes
Georgetown
Seaford
Rehoboth
Bay
Nanticoke
Indian River
Bay
Laurel
MARYLAND

0   10 Mi.
0   10 Km.
© Rand McNally
N-CUS24800-P1- -1- -1

The Way It Was . . .
A Famous Family

In 1799 the du Pont family
left France and settled in
Delaware. The family originally
ran a small but very successful
gunpowder plant. Many
members of the du Pont
family had a keen
business sense.
Generations of du
Ponts went on to
manufacture chemicals
and chemical products.
The products devel-
oped include rubber,
nylon, and cellophane.
Today tourists can visit
the family's former
houses, including
Winterthur, which is
now a museum.

*The Winterthur
Museum displays
decorative items
from the years
1640 to 1860.*

*During the first weekend in May,
Old Dover Days celebrate the
founding of Delware's capital city.*

*On summer weekends, thousands
of vacationers crowd the sandy
ocean shore at Rehoboth Beach.*

Nicknames

Delaware's nickname, the "First
State," comes from the fact that it
was the first state in the Union.
But it has had other nicknames as
well. Delaware has been called the
Diamond State because, like a
diamond, it is small but valuable.
A Delaware militia captain in the
Revolutionary War named his victorious men Blue Hen Chickens
after the fierce fighting birds, giving the state another nickname,
the "Blue Hen State."

State Facts

Delaware Flag

Blue Hen Chicken

Peach Blossom

American Holly

Nickname
First State

Capital
Dover

Area
1,954 square miles
(5,061 sq km)
Rank: 49th

Population
830,400
Rank: 45th

Statehood
December 7, 1787
1st state admitted

Principal River
Delaware River

Highest Point
448 feet (137 m),
in New Castle County

Song
"Our Delaware"

Motto
Liberty and
independence

Famous People
Annie Jump Cannon,
E. I. du Pont,
Howard Pyle

1899
Delaware Corporation
Law passed

1951
Opening of Delaware
Memorial Bridge

200 YEARS

1987
Delaware's
bicentennial

2002
Ruth Ann Minner becomes
state's first woman governor

1933
State capitol
completed

1971
Coastal Zone Act prohibits
industrial construction in
coastal areas

1990
Delaware's population
exceeds 666,000

FLORIDA

The name *Florida* means "flowery" in Spanish, and more than 3,000 varieties of flowers grow in this sunny state. Florida also has an abundance of fruits, especially oranges. The state's many other appealing features include 1,800 miles (2,880 kilometers) of warm, sandy beaches. It's no wonder that about 40 million tourists visit Florida each year.

The Land of Florida

Florida is largely a peninsula — a piece of land almost completely surrounded by water. Most of the land is low and flat; in fact, Florida has the lowest average elevation of all the states. The Everglades, one of the largest swamp regions in the world, is Florida's most famous natural feature. This area is home to alligators, crocodiles, panthers, bobcats, sea turtles, and beautiful birds. Off the state's southern tip, 42 bridges connect a strip of islands. These islands are known as the Florida Keys. Bridges aren't the only way to get from island to island: Glass-bottomed boats allow a closer look at tropical fish, coral, and even shipwrecks.

Ocean Drive in Miami Beach

Protected Animals in Florida

- **Alligators**
  Alligator farms through-out Florida do their part to help preserve these reptiles.

- **Manatee**
  There are only about 2,000 of these giant sea mammals left in Florida's waters.

- **Panthers**
  Rare Florida black panthers occasionally can be spotted in the Everglades.

The Everglades teem with a variety of wildlife, including alligators and roseate spoonbills.

Cannons once defended Spanish forts in Florida.

Timeline

1513
Ponce de León explores Florida

1528
Pánfilo de Narváez explores Tampa Bay

1565
St. Augustine, first permanent European settlement in North America, is founded

1700s
Creeks settle alongside other Native Americans and become known as Seminoles

1763
Spain cedes Florida to Britain

1783
Britain returns Florida to Spain

1817
First Seminole War begins

State Facts

Florida Flag

Mockingbird

Orange Blossom

Sabal Palm

Nickname
Sunshine State

Capital
Tallahassee

Area
53,927 square miles
(139,670 sq km)
Rank: 26th

Population
17,397,200
Rank: 4th

Statehood
March 3, 1845
27th state admitted

Principal Rivers
Apalachicola River,
St. Johns River,
Suwannee River

Highest Point
345 feet (105 m),
in Walton County

Motto
In God we trust

Song
"Old Folks at Home"

Famous People
Pat Boone,
Chris Evert,
Zora Neale Hurston,
Janet Reno

A Great Place to Visit and Stay

Every year, people who are tired of winter weather in the north come to Florida to relax in the sunshine. Tourists who want to do something more active can visit several large theme parks. Circuses travel to Florida in the winter, too, making their home in Sarasota. Some people who come to Florida to visit decide to stay. Senior citizens who move to Florida from other states make up a large part of Florida's population. In fact, one out of five Floridians is a senior citizen.

The first passenger train to Key West

The Way It Was . . . Riding the Rails

In the 1880s, two different railroad developers had the same idea: to build a railroad along the coast of Florida. Trains could then carry cargo, like oranges and grapefruits, up the coast to the northern states. More importantly, the railroad could bring northern tourists to Florida! Henry Plant built his railroad along the west coast, down to Tampa, and lined it with resorts and hotels. Henry Flagler did the same thing on the east coast, stopping at Palm Beach. Eventually, Flagler extended his train line all the way south to Key West. By the year 1900, people could explore Florida from top to bottom by rail.

The space shuttle Discovery

1821
Florida becomes part of U.S.

1914
World's first airline flies from St. Petersburg to Tampa

1969
Apollo 11 launched from Cape Canaveral

2000
Florida voting controversy delays presidential election results

1835
Second Seminole War begins

1845
Florida becomes 27th state

1947
Florida Everglades National Park is created

1962
First manned space flights launched from Cape Canaveral

1971
Disney World opens

1992
Hurricane Andrew rips through Miami area

2004
Four hurricanes strike state

GEORGIA

Georgia, the last of the original 13 colonies, was named for England's King George II. This southern state is the largest state east of the Mississippi River. In Georgia, visitors can see both old and new. Historic Georgia is on display in the Savannah area, a place with plantation mansions, peach orchards, and acres of green lawns. Modern Georgia is represented by Atlanta, a fast-growing metropolis filled with gleaming skyscrapers.

Atlanta

Atlanta is one of the fastest growing cities in the United States. It is considered the financial hub of the Southeast, and its airport is one of the busiest

in the country. Atlanta has many skyscrapers, yet it is also the most densely wooded city in the United States. Nearby Stone Mountain has images of Confederate leaders carved into its side. Atlanta played a key role in the civil rights movement. Martin Luther King, Jr. was born in Atlanta in 1929 and spent much of his life there, working toward his goals of ensuring peace, freedom, and equal rights for all people.

The Atlanta skyline

Savannah, the oldest city in Georgia, is an important port at the mouth of the Savannah River.

Peanuts

Peanuts, sometimes called "goobers" by people who live in Georgia, are the top product grown in the state. Rich soil and warm weather help Georgia farmers produce more than $1^{1}/_{2}$ billion pounds of peanuts every year, half of which are made into peanut butter. Peanuts are also crushed and used to make other things, such as peanut oil. Peanuts are even found in shampoo and paint.

Timeline

1540
Hernando de Soto explores Georgia

1721
Fort King George built

1736
Augusta founded

1742
British defeat Spanish in Battle of Bloody Marsh

1777
First Georgia constitution adopted

1779
British capture Savannah

1782
British troops leave Georgia

1788
Georgia becomes fourth state

1793
Eli Whitney invents cotton gin near Savannah

1837
Terminus (now Atlanta) founded

Chattanooga
TENN. N.C.
Brasstown Bald
4,784 Ft. +
1,458 M.
Dalton
Hartwell Lake
APPALACHIAN MTS.
Rome
L. Sidney Lanier
Gainesville
J. Strom Thurmond Lake
Marietta
Athens
Atlanta
Decatur
SOUTH CAROLINA
ALABAMA
Carrollton
Lake Oconee
Augusta
Griffin
Savannah
West Point Lake
Lake Sinclair
La Grange
Milledgeville
Warm Springs
Macon
Columbus
Warner Robins
Flint
Oconee
Statesboro
Walter F. George Reservoir
Americus
Savannah
Altamaha
Albany
Tifton
ST. SIMONS ISLAND
Moultrie
Waycross
Brunswick
ATLANTIC OCEAN
Chattahoochee
Lake Seminole
Valdosta
St. Marys
St. Marys
Thomasville
FLORIDA
Okefenokee Swamp
Jacksonville

0 10 20 30 Mi.
0   20   40 Km.
© Rand McNally
N-CUS25100-P1- -1-1-1

From Mountains to Swampland

Thick forests cover the slopes of the beautiful Blue Ridge Mountains in northern Georgia. The Piedmont, a region of gently rolling hills, occupies much of central Georgia. The southern Piedmont slopes down to meet the coastal plain, the largest and lowest part of the state. Farms on the coastal plain produce peanuts, sweet potatoes, and many other crops. Okefenokee Swamp is also located there. The swamp's 700 square miles (1,820 square kilometers) are now a wildlife refuge, home to the largest alligators in North America.

Sandhill cranes, river otters, bears, and bowfin fish all live in Okefenokee Swamp.

The Way It Was . . .
The Little White House

Franklin Delano Roosevelt, president of the United States from 1933 to 1945, spent a lot of time at Warm Springs, named for its natural springs and year-round warm weather.

President Roosevelt waves to onlookers as his train departs on April 28, 1940.

In 1921, Roosevelt had contracted polio, a disease that caused him severe pain and partial paralysis. Like many other polio patients, he felt relief when he swam at Warm Springs. In 1926, Roosevelt bought the springs and surrounding land, where he set up the Georgia Warm Springs Foundation to provide low-cost treatment for polio patients. In 1938, Roosevelt founded the organization that would come to be known as the March of Dimes. Whenever possible during his presidency, Roosevelt liked to retreat to the "Little White House" at Warm Springs, and it was there that he died in 1945.

State Facts

Georgia Flag

Brown Thrasher

Cherokee Rose

Live Oak

Nickname
Peach State

Capital
Atlanta

Area
57,906 square miles
(149,976 sq km)
Rank: 21st

Population
8,829,400
Rank: 9th

Statehood
January 2, 1788
4th state admitted

Principal Rivers
Chattahoochee River,
Flint River,
Savannah River

Highest Point
Brasstown Bald,
4,784 feet (1,458 m)

Motto
Wisdom, justice,
and moderation

Song
"Georgia on My Mind"

Famous People
Jimmy Carter,
Martin Luther King, Jr.,
Margaret Mitchell,
Julia Roberts

1868
Atlanta becomes state capital

1912
Girl Scouts founded in Savannah

1976
Jimmy Carter, former Georgia governor, elected president

2001
State flag is replaced

1864
Union General William T. Sherman burns Atlanta

1886
Coca-Cola invented

1964
Martin Luther King, Jr. receives Nobel Peace Prize

1996
Atlanta hosts 100th anniversary of modern Olympic Games

2002
Jimmy Carter receives Nobel Peace Prize

HAWAII

The name *Hawaii* is believed to have come from a legendary Polynesian homeland called Hawaiki. Centuries ago, Hawaii's inhabitants called their islands *Ke Ao Nani*, meaning "the beautiful world." As a state, Hawaii is unique in several ways. It's the only state that is not part of the North American continent. The chain of islands that make up Hawaii stretches across 1,523 miles (2,451 kilometers) of Pacific Ocean, far away from the other states. Hawaii is also the youngest and the southernmost state. And it's the only state that was once an independent monarchy.

The Islands of Hawaii

The Hawaiian islands are actually the peaks of huge undersea volcanoes. Most of the volcanoes are no longer active, but some continue to erupt. The sparkling black sand covering some Hawaiian beaches formed when hot lava from the volcanoes flowed into the ocean. Of the 132 Hawaiian islands, 124 are too tiny for people to live on. The state's eight main islands lie at the southeast end of the chain. People call the island of Hawai'i, which is the largest in area, the Big Island. Most of the state's people, however, live on O'ahu.

Kilauea, a volcanic crater on the island of Hawai'i, sends steady streams of lava seaward.

Hawaii's Economy

Tourism is Hawaii's largest industry. The sandy beaches, year-round mild climate, and spectacular volcanic scenery make Hawaii a great vacation spot. Hawaii's economy once depended on sugarcane and pineapples, and these are still important products, as are flowers, beef and dairy cattle, coffee, and macadamia nuts. Hawaii's location has made it a major center of United States military activities. Army, Air Force, Navy, and Marine bases are all found in Hawaii and employ both civilians and military personnel. The cost of living in Hawaii is high compared to most other states. Since Hawaii is remote and has little manufacturing, many items must be brought across the ocean on ships or planes, which raises the costs of these goods.

Diamond Head, the crater of an extinct volcano, looms over Waikiki Beach on the island of O'ahu.

Timeline

1778
Captain James Cook explores Hawaii

1795
King Kamehameha unites Hawaiian Islands

1820
Missionaries from New England arrive and organize schools

1835
First sugarcane fields planted on island of Kauai

1840
First written constitution

1893
Queen Liliuokalani deposed

1894
Sanford B. Dole becomes Hawaii's first and only president

1898
U.S. annexes Hawaii

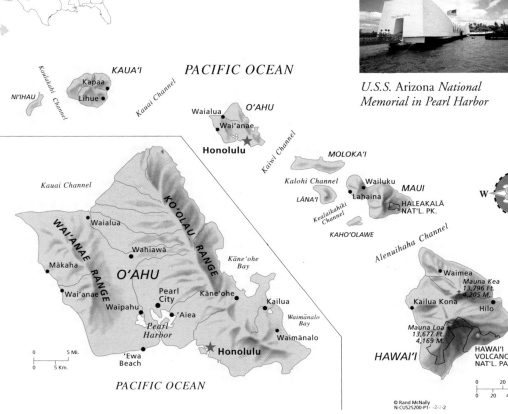

PACIFIC OCEAN

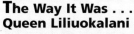

PACIFIC OCEAN

U.S.S. Arizona *National Memorial in Pearl Harbor*

State Facts

Hawaii Flag

Nene (Hawaiian Goose)

Yellow Hibiscus

Kukui (Candlenut)

Nickname
Aloha State

Capital
Honolulu

Area
6,423 square miles
(16,636 sq km)
Rank: 47th

Population
1,262,800
Rank: 42nd

Statehood
August 21, 1959
50th state admitted

Principal River
Wailuku River (Hawai'i)

Highest Point
Mauna Kea (Hawai'i),
13,796 feet (4,205 m)

Motto
Ua mau ke ea o ka aina i ka pono
(The life of the land is perpetuated in righteousness)

Song
"Hawaii Ponoi"

Famous People
Don Ho,
Daniel K. Inouye,
Bette Midler,
Ellison Onizuka

The Way It Was . . . Queen Liliuokalani

Queen Liliuokalani

When Liliuokalani became queen of independent Hawaii in 1891, she faced a nation in crisis. For more than a century, Americans had been coming to Hawaii. The Hawaiian economy was controlled by Americans who owned sugarcane plantations on the islands. The Americans had forced Liliuokalani's late brother, King Kalakaua, to accept a constitution that gave the Americans much political power. Queen Liliuokalani was determined to restore native self-government. She proposed a new constitution and tried to rally her people behind the slogan "Hawaii for the Hawaiians." In 1893, a group of Americans, supported by United States Marines, staged a revolt. The queen was forced to surrender authority. Imprisoned in Iolani Palace in Honolulu, she wrote the haunting song "Aloha Oe" ("Farewell to Thee"). After her release, she lived as a private citizen until her death in 1917. By then, Hawaii had become a United States territory.

People and Languages

The first settlers of Hawaii were Polynesians who came from islands farther south in the Pacific Ocean. They arrived in huge canoes as early as 2,000 years ago and were ruled by local chiefs until King Kamehameha I united the groups in the late 1700s. Their descendants, known as native Hawaiians, make up only a small part of the state's population. But their culture is alive and well. For example, Hawaii has two official languages: English and Hawaiian. The Hawaiian alphabet consists of 12 letters: vowels *a, e, i, o,* and *u,* and consonants *h, k, l, m, n, p,* and *w.* The Hawaiian word *aloha,* the basis of the state's nickname, has several meanings, including "welcome," "love," and "farewell."

1908
Building of Pearl Harbor naval base begins

1941
Japanese attack Pearl Harbor

1978
Hawaiian language is legalized

1993
U.S. government formally apologizes for taking over Hawaii in 1893

1900
Hawaii becomes a territory

1934
President Franklin D. Roosevelt visits

1959
Hawaii becomes 50th state

1992
Hurricane Iniki strikes

1994
First observation made by Keck 1 telescope on Mauna Kea

IDAHO

Although it may be based on a Native American word or phrase, *Idaho* is an invented name. But there is nothing invented or artificial about Idaho's scenic beauty. The state is a natural wonderland of lofty mountains, lush forests, sparkling lakes, and rivers whose waters rush and tumble through churning rapids and plunging waterfalls. It's no surprise that Idaho attracts thousands of sightseers and other outdoor enthusiasts every season of the year.

A tranquil mountain cabin in the shadow of the Sawtooth Range

Craters of the Moon National Park

Geography

On a map of the United States, Idaho's odd shape makes it stand out from its mostly rectangular neighbors. Various ranges of the Rocky Mountains — with intriguing names such as Bitterroot, Sawtooth, and Lost River — cover much of the state. In the southern part of the state, the Snake River forms a loop that looks something like a necklace. The land on each side of the river is Idaho's only flat region, and about 70 percent of Idaho's people live there. The area is naturally dry, but dams built on the Snake River allow farmers to irrigate the fertile soil and produce bumper harvests of Idaho's most famous product: potatoes.

Economy

Idaho produces about one-fourth of the United States' potato crop and about two-thirds of the country's processed potatoes. Idaho farmers and ranchers also raise barley, wheat, sugar beets, alfalfa, beef and dairy cattle, and sheep. Mining has played an important role in Idaho's history. Discoveries of silver and gold in the 1800s brought a wave of prospectors. Later, some mines closed down and people abandoned the boomtowns that had sprung up nearby. Nevertheless, Idaho continues to be a leader in silver production.

Harvesting barley

Timeline

1805
Meriwether Lewis and William Clark are first white men to travel through region

1810
Fort Henry built

1819
Spain gives up claim to Idaho

1834
Fort Hall established

1836
Lapwai Mission Station established near Lewiston

1848
Cataldo Mission established

1855
Mormons build Idaho's first irrigation system

1860
First permanent settlement, Franklin, established

1860
Gold discovered in Idaho

1863
Idaho becomes a territory

Cross-country skiers glide through spectacular mountain scenery in Sun Valley.

Skiing Idaho

Mountains blanketed with winter snow make Idaho a skier's dream. The state's best-known ski resort, Sun Valley, dates from the 1930s. The resort has nearly 60 ski runs, as well as many cross-country ski trails.

A mountain man with pack ponies and rifle at the ready

The Way It Was . . . Mountain Men

In the early 1800s, top hats made of glossy beaver fur were the height of fashion for men in the eastern United States and Europe. Beaver pelts commanded high prices, and fur companies hired men to go into the western wilderness to trap beavers. The trappers, also known as mountain men, lived rough, lonely lives most of the year. Each summer, though, they left their isolated mountain homes to gather at a large meeting known as the rendezvous. There the mountain men sold pelts, bought supplies, and swapped wild tales of their adventures. One popular rendezvous site was the shore of Bear Lake, on the border between present-day Idaho and Utah. The last rendezvous took place in 1837. By then, silk was more popular than fur for top hats, and the beaver was almost extinct due to excessive hunting. The heyday of the colorful mountain men was over.

Idaho fly fishermen cast into the state's many streams in pursuit of steelhead, cutthroat, and rainbow trout.

State Facts

Idaho Flag

Mountain Bluebird

Syringa

Western White Pine

Nickname
Gem State

Capital
Boise

Area
82,747 square miles
(214,314 sq km)
Rank: 11th

Population
1,393,300
Rank: 39th

Statehood
July 3, 1890
43rd state admitted

Principal River
Snake River

Highest Point
Borah Peak,
12,662 feet (3,859 m)

Motto
Esto perpetua
(Let it be perpetual)

Song
"Here We Have Idaho"

Famous People
Gutzon Borglum,
Ezra Pound,
Sacagawea,
Picabo Street

1877
End of Nez Percé
Indian War

1890
Idaho becomes
43rd state

1910
Forest fires ravage
northern Idaho

1936
Sun Valley ski
resort opens

1976
Teton River Dam bursts

1992
State capitol catches fire,
causing $3.2 million in damage

2004
Nez Perce tribal claim to Snake
River water rights is resolved

ILLINOIS

The midwestern state of Illinois gets its name from a Native American group called the Illiniwek. The French explorers who first set foot in the region in the later 1600s named it after these Indians. Today about 80 percent of the land is used for farming, but 80 percent of the state's residents live in urban areas, primarily the city of Chicago and its suburbs.

Chicago

Chicago is the third-largest city in the United States and home to some amazing achievements. The Sears Tower, which stands 1,454 feet (440 meters) tall, is one of the world's tallest buildings.

On a clear day, you can see Indiana, Michigan, and Wisconsin from the observation deck on the building's top floor. O'Hare International Airport, where a plane takes off or lands every 23 seconds, is the world's busiest airport. Chicago is also home to the El, a system of elevated trains. Its tracks snake through the city, moving many of the city's nearly three million residents from place to place.

Lakefront buildings in Chicago

Navy Pier and Chicago's dramatic skyline

Land of Lincoln

Although Abraham Lincoln was born in Kentucky, his name is closely associated with Illinois. Lincoln moved to Springfield, the capital, when he was a young attorney. It was in Illinois, while campaigning for the United States Senate in 1858, that Lincoln took part in a series of famous debates with Senator Stephen A. Douglas. Lincoln won the debates, but not the Senate seat. In 1860, Lincoln was elected president. A few weeks after his inauguration, the Civil War began. In 1865, Lincoln was killed by an assassin's bullet while attending a play at Ford's Theatre in Washington, D.C.

Timeline

1699
First permanent settlement established in Cahokia

1809
Congress organizes Illinois Territory

1832
Black Hawk War

1847
McCormick reaper plant opens in Chicago

1673
Jacques Marquette and Louis Jolliet explore Illinois region

1763
British cede area to France

1818
Illinois becomes 21st state

1839
Springfield becomes state capital

Soybeans, which come from these small plants, are used to produce a variety of goods, from margarine to printing inks.

Illinois Farmland

Illinois produces a variety of crops. The richness of the soil is due largely to minerals left behind by melting glaciers thousands of years ago. Illinois is the largest producer of soybeans in the United States. In addition to soybeans, farmers grow corn, wheat, oats, barley, rye, and sorghum. They also raise hogs, cattle, and chickens.

Crowds gather at the opening day ceremonies.

The Way It Was . . . The World's Columbian Exposition

In 1871, much of Chicago burned to the ground in a tragic fire. Hundreds of people died, and thousands were left homeless. Some wondered if the city would ever be the same. That question was answered in 1893 with the opening of the World's Columbian Exposition in Chicago's Jackson Park. Visitors marveled at the Ferris wheel, which stood an amazing 264 feet (80 meters) tall. Classically designed buildings lined Michigan Avenue while leaving a clear view of Lake Michigan glittering in the east. Many of the buildings, including the Art Institute, are still in use. Having risen from the ashes of the 1871 fire, Chicago became a world-class city.

Galena, in the northwest corner of Illinois, is known for its lovely Civil War-era mansions and buildings.

State Facts

Illinois Flag

Cardinal

Native Violet

White Oak

Nickname
Land of Lincoln

Capital
Springfield

Area
55,584 square miles
(143,962 sq km)
Rank: 24th

Population
12,713,600
Rank: 5th

Statehood
December 3, 1818
21st state admitted

Principal Rivers
Illinois River,
Mississippi River,
Ohio River

Highest Point
Charles Mound,
1,235 feet (376 m)

Motto
State sovereignty—
national union

Song
"Illinois"

Famous People
Walt Disney,
Harrison Ford,
Ernest Hemingway,
Ronald Reagan,
Carl Sandburg

1858
Lincoln-Douglas debates

1886
Haymarket Riot erupts during labor rally

1933
World's Fair opens in Chicago

1992
Carol Moseley Braun becomes first female African American U.S. senator

1871
Great Chicago Fire

1889
Jane Addams opens Hull House

1893
World's Columbian Exposition opens in Chicago

1973
Sears Tower completed

1991-1998
Chicago Bulls win six NBA championships

2003
Governor George Ryan commutes death sentences for all Illinois prison inmates

INDIANA

Though many state names come from Native American words, *Indiana* is an English word describing an area once populated by "Indians." Long before Native Americans lived in Indiana, glaciers covered nearly three-fourths of the state. When they melted, the glaciers left behind flat layers of rich soil in the state's central region and low hills in the northern region. Glaciers did not cover the southern part of the state, which is known for caves and limestone

The Golden Dome overlooks the University of Notre Dame campus.

quarries. Perhaps Indiana's most special feature is its Lake Michigan shoreline. Sand dunes line the lake and are protected as part of the Indiana Dunes National Lakeshore.

Farming and Industry

Central Indiana's flat, fertile fields yield crops of corn, soybeans, wheat, and tomatoes. Farmers raise livestock as well — mainly hogs, but also cattle, sheep, chickens, and turkeys. Cities such as Gary and Hammond produce steel, Elkhart is known for producing musical instruments, and Fort Wayne is a large maker of diamond tools. In the early 20th century Indianapolis was a major car manufacturer, which is why the famous International Motor Speedway was built there. Now the capital city is best known for producing pharmaceuticals, machinery, and telephones.

Johnny Appleseed

There are many folk tales that have come out of the United States, many of which are no more than legends of an active frontier imagination. This is not the case with John Chapman, who is better known as Johnny Appleseed. Chapman, a dedicated naturalist, traveled the Ohio River valley planting apple seeds along the way. He is credited with establishing orchards and tree nurseries across the Midwest. In 1845, Chapman, traveling to an orchard in northern Indiana, was stricken with pneumonia and died not long after.

The Indianapolis 500 auto race takes place every year on Memorial Day weekend.

Johnny Appleseed prepares the ground for planting apple seeds.

Timeline

1679
René-Robert Cavelier, Sieur de la Salle, explores Indiana

1731
Vincennes becomes site of first permanent settlement

1794
Fort Wayne founded

1800
Congress establishes Indiana Territory

1811
Battle of Tippecanoe

1816
Indiana becomes 19th state

1824
Indianapolis becomes state capital

1825
Robert Owens founds New Harmony

1832
Work begins on Wabash and Erie Canal

Hoosiers

People who live in Indiana are known as Hoosiers. Historians and Indianans have several theories about how this unusual nickname came to be. Some say it came from Indiana settlers who gruffly anwered "Who's yere?" when a visitor knocked on the door. Another theory points to Sam Hoosier. In 1826 he hired many men from Indiana to work on a canal being dug near Louisville, Kentucky. Soon the Indiana workers were known as "Hoosier's men." Eventually, as this theory goes, all Indiana residents became known as Hoosiers.

William Henry Harrison (1783-1841)

The Way It Was . . . The Shortest Presidency in History

When William Henry Harrison was chosen to be governor of the Indiana Territory in 1800, many Native Americans and few white settlers lived there. Native Americans resisted the movement of more white settlers into the territory, but in 1811 Harrison and a small army defeated them at the Battle of Tippecanoe, near present-day Lafayette. In 1840 Harrison was elected the ninth president of the United States. The election slogan "Tippecanoe and Tyler too!" reminded voters that Harrison was once a victorious military leader (John Tyler was the vice president). On inauguration day — March 4, 1841 — it was cold and rainy, but Harrison refused to wear a hat and overcoat during his speech. He caught pneumonia and died a month later, on April 4. He was the first president to die in office, and he also served the shortest term.

Grasses hold fragile sand dunes in place along the Indiana Dunes National Lakeshore.

State Facts

Indiana Flag

Cardinal

Peony

Tulip Tree

Nickname
Hoosier State

Capital
Indianapolis

Area
35,867 square miles
(92,895 sq km)
Rank: 38th

Population
6,237,600
Rank: 14th

Statehood
December 11, 1816
19th state admitted

Principal Rivers
Ohio River,
Wabash River

Highest Point
1,257 feet (383 m),
in Wayne County

Motto
Crossroads of America

Song
"On the Banks of the
Wabash, Far Away"

Famous People
Larry Bird,
Virgil "Gus" Grissom,
William Henry Harrison,
Jane Pauley, Cole Porter,
Dan Quayle

1845
John "Johnny Appleseed" Chapman dies

1911
First Indianapolis 500-mile Memorial Day race

1988
State lottery approved

2004
Severe spring storms and floods cause statewide damage

1850
National Road completed across Indiana

1956
Indiana Toll Road completed

1988
Dan Quayle becomes vice president of the United States

IOWA

An Iowa farm

State capitol in Des Moines

The Iowa Caucus

Every four years, Iowa plays an important role in the campaign for the presidency of the United States. Before other states begin selecting delegates, who pledge their votes to candidates at a national convention, Iowa holds what is called a caucus. In a caucus, registered voters get together to talk over issues as well as to discuss the candidates. In order to earn votes, presidential candidates listen carefully to what Iowans have to say.

The name *Iowa* comes from a Native American word that means "beautiful land." Bordering Iowa's picturesque land to the east and west are two mighty rivers — the Mississippi on the east and the Missouri on the west. Both rivers provide irrigation and transportation for crops grown throughout the state.

Feeding the Country

If you look down at Iowa from an airplane, you will see what look like carpets of corn, hay, and wheat. That's because more than 90 percent of the land in Iowa is farmland. Warm summer temperatures, lots of rain, fertile soil, and a growing season of more than 140 days make Iowa ideal for farming. Iowa is the country's leading producer of corn. The tallest cornstalk on record was grown near Washington, Iowa. Measuring 31 feet (nine meters), the cornstalk was as tall as a three-story building! Iowa farmers also raise livestock. More hogs are raised in Iowa than in any other state. Although Iowa has plentiful farmland, it does not have an abundance of farmers. More than half of Iowans live in the state's cities and towns.

Trees surround a burial mound.

Effigy Mounds

Effigy Mounds National Monument, near the town of Marquette, is the site of prehistoric burial mounds. The mounds, some of which are about 300 feet (90 meters) long and are shaped like animals, sit on a bluff in northeastern Iowa overlooking the Mississippi River.

Timeline

1788
Julian Dubuque becomes first white settler

1830
Dr. Isaac Galland establishes first school

1846
Iowa becomes 29th state

1857
Des Moines becomes state capital

1673
Jacques Marquette and Louis Jolliet claim land for France

1803
U.S. acquires Iowa through Louisiana Purchase

1832
Native American leader Black Hawk defeated

1856
First bridge across Mississippi River built at Davenport

MINNESOTA

SOUTH DAKOTA

Osceola Co.
1,670 Ft.
509 M.

Spencer

Decorah

Mason City

Shell Rock

Des Moines

Storm Lake

Sioux City

Ft. Dodge

Waterloo

Dubuque

WISCONSIN

ILLINOIS

Big Sioux

Missouri

Carroll

Boone

Ames

Marshalltown

Cedar Rapids

Clinton

NEBRASKA

Newton

Iowa City

Davenport

Bettendorf

Rock Island

Des Moines

Lake Red Rock

Oskaloosa

Cedar

Council Bluffs

Des Moines

Ottumwa

Shenandoah

Burlington
Fort Madison

MISSOURI

Keokuk

© Rand McNally
N-CUS25600-P1- -1-1--1

0   25   50 Mi.
0   35   70 Km.

Women's Right to Vote

Carrie Chapman Catt, an Iowa teacher, played a leading role in helping women gain suffrage — the right to vote. In 1900, Catt succeeded Susan B. Anthony as president of the National American Woman Suffrage Association. After women gained voting rights in 1920, Catt founded the League of Women Voters, a group that still influences politics today.

Mississippi River at McGregor

The Way it Was . . . The Amana Colonies

A community kitchen in the Amana colonies

In 1855, a group of German immigrants who had been persecuted in Germany for their religious beliefs and refusal to serve as soldiers founded the seven Amana colonies in Iowa. The colonies were actually small villages. The Amanites had no use for money because everyone worked together to achieve common goals. Several families shared one large house, and community kitchens fed all of the colonists. In addition to making food, the Amanites produced their own clothes and furniture. After almost 80 years of this way of life, the Amana Society decided to make major changes. The Amanites began to dress like most other Americans and to enjoy such conveniences as indoor plumbing, electricity, and cars. However, the changes in lifestyle did not alter the high level of craftsmanship in the colonies. Even today, fine furniture, fabrics, and baked goods are made with pride in Amana Colonies.

State Facts

Iowa Flag

Eastern Goldfinch

Wild Rose

Oak

Nickname
Hawkeye State

Capital
Des Moines

Area
55,869 square miles
(144,700 sq km)
Rank: 23rd

Population
2,954,500
Rank: 30th

Statehood
December 28, 1846
29th state admitted

Principal Rivers
Des Moines River,
Mississippi River,
Missouri River

Highest Point
1,670 feet (509 m),
in Osceola County

Motto
Our liberties we prize
and our rights we
will maintain

Song
"The Song of Iowa"

Famous People
Herbert Hoover,
John Wayne,
Grant Wood

1867
First railroad service begins

1913
Keokuk Dam completed

1928
Iowa native Herbert Hoover elected president

1958
University of Iowa physicist discovers Van Allen radiation belt

1985
State lottery established

1993
Heavy rains cause floods and $2 billion in damage

1996
Iowa celebrates 150th birthday

2002
Iowa leads nation in production of pork, corn, soybeans, and eggs

KANSAS

Kansas is a rectangular state in the middle of the United States. In fact, the exact geographic center of the continental United States is near the town of Lebanon in Kansas. Now home to 2.5 million people, the state was named after the Kansa — Native Americans who once lived in the area and whose name means "people of the south wind." Viewed at ground level, Kansas appears flat, but is actually slanted, increasing in elevation from east to west. For a long time, Kansas's harsh weather discouraged many would-be settlers. Those who chose to come and stay, however, found their reward in the wide open spaces and rich soil.

Pioneers and Soddies

In 1854, the Kansas-Nebraska Act opened the Kansas territory to settlers, encouraging many people to build homes and raise families in the area. Compared to many states, Kansas has few trees. The settlers who poured into Kansas faced a shortage of wood for building homes. Their solution was to build soddies — small houses made of slabs of grass-covered earth.

Kansas is the top wheat producer in the United States.

Monument Rocks, also known as Chalk Pyramids, in western Kansas

A wagon train crosses the prairie.

Buffalo and Other Wildlife

Three hundred years ago, 70 million buffalo — also known by the name "bison" — roamed the land that would someday be Kansas. By the late 1800s, hunting had nearly wiped out the buffalo. Today small buffalo herds are protected in refuges throughout the state. Kansas's diverse wildlife also includes antelopes, pheasants, squirrel, and deer.

Timeline

1803
Kansas becomes part of U.S. through Louisiana Purchase

1827
Fort Leavenworth established

1860
Railroad reaches Kansas

1880
Kansas is first state to enact constitutional prohibition of alcohol

1541
Francisco Vásquez de Coronado explores Kansas

1821
Santa Fe Trail through Kansas established

1854
Kansas-Nebraska Act creates Kansas territory, opens area to settlers

1861
Kansas becomes 34th state

1903
State capitol completed

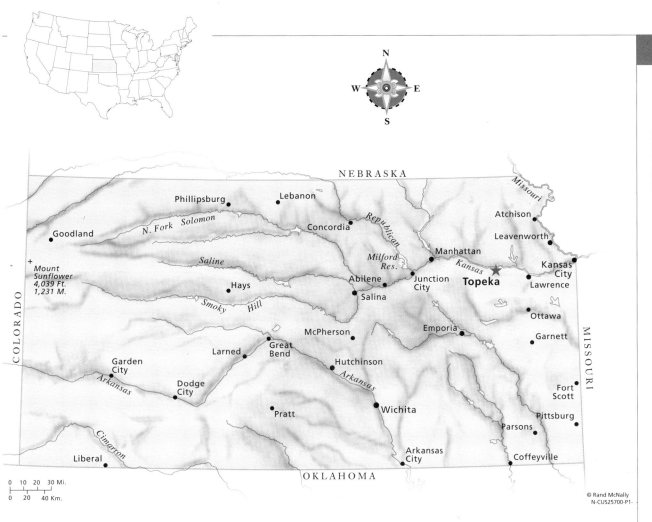

NEBRASKA

Phillipsburg
Lebanon
Atchison
Goodland
N. Fork Solomon
Concordia
Republican
Leavenworth
Missouri
Saline
Milford Res.
Manhattan
Kansas
Kansas City
Mount Sunflower 4,039 Ft. 1,231 M.
Hays
Abilene
Junction City
Topeka
Lawrence
Smoky Hill
Salina
COLORADO
McPherson
Emporia
Ottawa
Garnett
Larned
Great Bend
Hutchinson
MISSOURI
Garden City
Arkansas
Dodge City
Arkansas
Fort Scott
Pratt
Wichita
Pittsburg
Parsons
Cimarron
Arkansas City
Coffeyville
Liberal

OKLAHOMA

0 10 20 30 Mi.
0 20 40 Km.

© Rand McNally
N-CUS25700-P1-

State Facts

KANSAS

Kansas Flag

Western Meadowlark

Native Sunflower

Cottonwood

Nickname
Sunflower State

Capital
Topeka

Area
81,815 square miles
(211,900 sq km)
Rank: 13th

Population
2,735,500
Rank: 33rd

Statehood
January 29, 1861
34th state admitted

Principal Rivers
Arkansas River,
Kansas River

Highest Point
Mount Sunflower,
4,039 feet (1,231 m)

Motto
As astra per aspera
(To the stars
through difficulty)

Song
"Home on the Range"

Famous People
Robert Dole,
Amelia Earhart,
Dwight Eisenhower,
Melissa Etheridge,
Nancy Kassebaum

Amelia Earhart waves from the cockpit of her plane.

Pilots and Planes

Kansas has long played an important role in aviation. Amelia Earhart, a Kansas native, was the first woman in the United States to earn an airplane pilot's license. She was also the first woman to fly alone across the Atlantic Ocean, in 1932. Earhart mysteriously disappeared with her navigator during an attempted flight around the world in 1937. Later, airplane production became big business in Kansas, where more than half the country's military and commercial planes were produced. In addition, the city of Wichita is home to McConnell Air Force Base, a major military installation.

The Way It Was . . . Dodge City

Dodge City has become a symbol of America's Wild West. Beginning in the 1870s, Dodge City was called the "wickedest little city" in the United States. Rowdy cowboys and buffalo hunters came to Dodge City to unwind. Drunkenness, disorder,

One cowboy dares another to fight him as the crowd looks on.

and crime were the result. Famous lawmen like Wyatt Earp and Bat Masterson tried to keep the "Cowboy Capital of the World" under control. Today, visitors to Dodge City can watch actors stage gunfights on a re-creation of the city's old main street.

1952
Dwight Eisenhower
elected president

1976
Mid-American All-Indian
Center opens

1985
Robert Dole becomes U.S.
Senate majority leader

1999
Tornado hits Wichita
and Haysville

1947
Tornado kills
169 people

1978
Nancy Kassebaum is first woman
elected to full U.S. Senate term
without succeeding a husband

1988
Drought devastates
Kansas farmland

1993
Heavy flooding causes
$475 million in crop
and property losses

KENTUCKY

Bordered by the Appalachian Mountains in the east and the Mississippi River in the west, Kentucky takes its name from a Cherokee word that means "land of tomorrow." The state is nicknamed the Bluegrass State for the silver-blue grass that blankets its fields and pastures.

Abraham Lincoln was born in Kentucky in 1809. His first home was a tiny cabin in the backwoods.

Cave of Wonders

Kentucky is home to Mammoth Cave National Park, a maze of underground passages that form the longest cave system in the world. The cave's five levels feature underground lakes, rivers, and waterfalls. Some rooms in the cave are so tall that they could hold a 12-story building. Thousands of years ago, people used the cave for shelter. Human remains found there are estimated to be more than 3,000 years old. Today the cave is home to many creatures, including tiny bats, blind beetles, white spiders, and eyeless fish, all of which have adapted to life in total darkness.

The Kentucky Derby

Each year on the first Saturday of May, Churchill Downs in Louisville hosts the Kentucky Derby, one of the most famous horse races in the world. The race covers 1¼ miles (two kilometers) and lasts only a few minutes, but Louisville celebrates for ten days leading up to the big event. Parades, concerts, parties, and fairs keep tourists and locals excited about the Derby. Horse farms throughout the Lexington and Louisville areas raise thoroughbreds that race in the Kentucky Derby.

The grandstand at Churchill Downs

Horse breeding and racing are long-standing Kentucky traditions.

Timeline

1750
Thomas Walker explores Kentucky

1767
Daniel Boone first explores Kentucky

1774
First permanent settlement, Harrodsburg, established

1775
Boonesborough founded

1787
The *Kentucky Gazette*, Kentucky's first newspaper, begins publication

1792
Kentucky becomes 15th state

1832
First railroad service begins in Kentucky

1860
Kentucky-born Abraha Lincoln elected preside

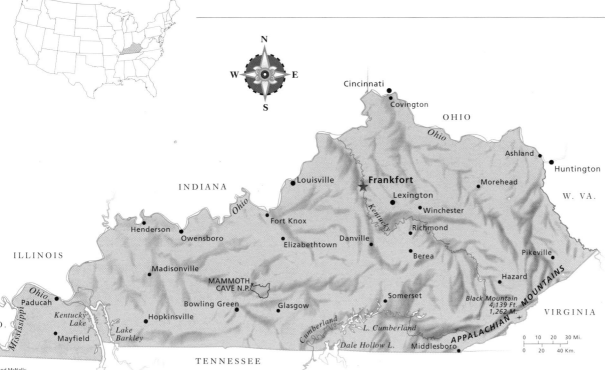

State Facts

Kentucky Flag

Cardinal

Goldenrod

Tulip Poplar

Nickname
Bluegrass State

Capital
Frankfort

Area
39,728 square miles
(102,895 sq km)
Rank: 36th

Population
4,145,900
Rank: 26th

Statehood
June 1, 1792
15th state admitted

Principal Rivers
Cumberland River,
Kentucky River,
Ohio River

Highest Point
Black Mountain,
4,139 feet (1,262 m)

Motto
United we stand,
divided we fall

Song
"My Old Kentucky Home"

Famous People
Muhammad Ali,
Kit Carson,
Abraham Lincoln,
Zachary Taylor

The Way It Was . . . Daniel Boone

Daniel Boone sees Kentucky for the first time.

In 1775, Daniel Boone led a group of settlers from North Carolina and Kentucky through the Cumberland Gap. The pioneers followed an old Native American trail that became known as the Wilderness Road, Kentucky's first road. Boone so loved Kentucky that he settled there with his family and built a fort called Boonesborough along the Kentucky River. Many other settlers followed to stake claims on the rich Kentucky land.

Shakers

Members of the religious group known as the Shakers came to live in Kentucky in the early 1800s. Although they lived simple lives as farmers, the innovative Shakers created some of the things we use today, including wooden clothespins. They also made beautifully crafted furniture. The distinct design of Shaker furniture is admired throughout the world today.

Shaker chair (right)

Fort Knox, site of a federal gold depository (far right)

1875
First Kentucky
Derby held

1891
Kentucky's 4th consti-
tution adopted

1909
State capitol opens in
Frankfort

1936
U.S. Treasury establishes gold
depository at Fort Knox

1944
Kentucky Dam
completed

1978
Federal law requires
strip-mine owners to
restore land

1995
Muhammad Ali
Museum opens

1998
Univ. of Kentucky Wildcats win
NCAA basketball championship

LOUISIANA

In 1682, the French explorer René-Robert Cavelier, Sieur de La Salle, claimed all of the Mississippi River Valley for France, whose king at the time was Louis XIV. La Salle dubbed the vast region Louisiana in honor of the king. Later the state we know as Louisiana was carved from the region. Bordering the Gulf of Mexico in the southern United States, modern-day Louisiana is famous for its colorful history, diverse population, great food, and lively music.

A Watery State

Averaging only 100 feet (30 meters) above sea level, Louisiana is one of the lowest states in the United States. Walls called levees, built along rivers, protect much of the state from flooding. Louisiana leads all states in commercial fishing, especially for shellfish such as shrimp and crab. Much of the catch is shipped elsewhere, but local restaurants offer tasty seafood. Louisiana has many bayous, or shallow channels with slow-moving water. Many kinds of birds, such as pelicans, herons, and egrets, live along the bayous and in the coastal marshes. More than 900,000 acres (365,000 hectares) of land in the state have been designated as a wildlife refuge.

The Creole Queen, *a Mississippi River paddle wheeler*

The unique architecture of the French Quarter is just one of the highlights of New Orleans.

New Orleans

New Orleans is known for its rich mix of Spanish, French, and African cultures. The city is dotted with lovely old buildings — many with ornate wrought-iron balconies — built when the Spanish and French ruled the area. New Orleans is famed for foods cooked in the Creole and Cajun styles. Creoles are descendants of French and Spanish settlers and African Americans brought as slaves, while Cajuns are descendants of settlers who came to Louisiana from the Acadia region of Canada and Maine. Today, visitors enjoy roaming the city's French Quarter, where jazz — invented by African-American musicians — pours out from restaurants and clubs. A cultural gem, New Orleans is also a major business center and port.

Timeline

1541
Hernando de Soto explores Louisiana

1682
René-Robert Cavelier, Sieur de La Salle, claims land for France

1699
Louisiana becomes a French royal colony

1718
New Orleans founded; named for Philippe, duc d'Orléans

1762
Louisiana ceded to Spain

1763
Acadians arrive from Canada and Maine

1800
Spain returns Louisiana to France

1803
French ruler Napoleon sells Louisiana to U.S.

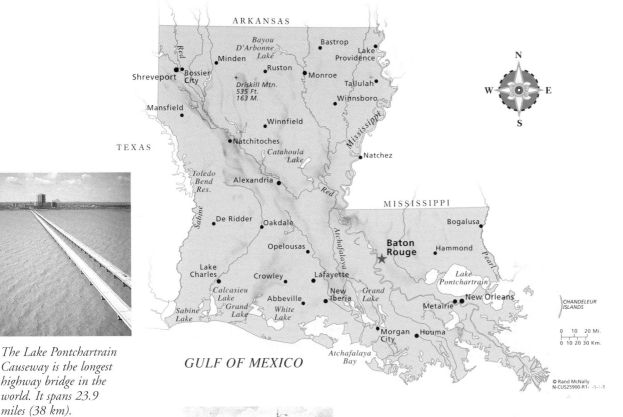

© Rand McNally
N-CUS25900-R1- -1-1-1

State Facts

Louisiana Flag

Eastern Brown Pelican

Magnolia

Bald Cypress

Nickname
Pelican State

Capital
Baton Rouge

Area
43,562 square miles
(112,825 sq km)
Rank: 33rd

Population
4,515,800
Rank: 24th

Statehood
April 30, 1812
18th state admitted

Principal Rivers
Mississippi River,
Red River,
Sabine River

Highest Point
Driskill Mountain,
535 feet (163 m)

Motto
Union, justice, and
confidence

Song
"Give Me Louisiana"

Famous People
Louis Armstrong,
Truman Capote,
Harry Connick, Jr.,
Mahalia Jackson,
Wynton Marsalis

The Lake Pontchartrain Causeway is the longest highway bridge in the world. It spans 23.9 miles (38 km).

The Battle of New Orleans took place in January 1815.

The Way It Was . . .
Jean Laffite

Jean Laffite lived in a magnificent home on an island near New Orleans, yet his businesses never seemed to do well. People suspected that Laffite was a pirate — a criminal who attacked ships and raided them for treasure. Louisiana's governor put up posters offering a reward for Laffite's capture. Laffite responded by putting up his own posters — with an even larger reward for the capture of the governor! Laffite surprised everyone when he and his followers became heroes by helping General Andrew Jackson defeat the British in the Battle of New Orleans during the War of 1812. After the battle, Laffite moved to Texas. In 1821 he sailed away. No one knows for sure what happened to him, but some have claimed that he left treasure buried all along the coast of the Gulf of Mexico.

Jazz

The music known as jazz was born in Louisiana in the late 1800s. It is sometimes called the only art form to originate in the United States. Jazz is influenced by African and other musical traditions. Today there are many kinds of jazz, including Dixieland, swing, and bebop.

1812
Louisiana becomes 18th state

1815
Battle of New Orleans

1850
Baton Rouge becomes state capital

1901
Oil discovered in Jennings

1928
Huey P. Long elected governor

1935
Former governor Long assassinated

1956
Causeway over Lake Pontchartrain opens

1984
Louisiana World Exposition held in New Orleans

1992
Hurricane Andrew devastates southern Louisiana

2004
Kathleen Babineaux Blanco becomes state's first woman governor

MAINE

Lighthouses are a familiar sight along the Maine coast.

Acadia National Park's Otter Cliffs rise sharply from the sea.

The name *Maine* is believed to come from the word "mainland," which early English explorers used to distinguish the continental part of the state from the offshore islands. Today Maine is the easternmost state, making up nearly half of the region known as New England. Maine's coast is famous not only for the bounty of fish it provides, but also for its rugged beauty.

From Sea to Forest

Maine is best known for two natural features: its long, rocky coastline and its vast pine forests. Maine's coast zigs and zags, forming countless bays and rocky points. The result is nearly 3,500 miles (5,600 kilometers) of twisting, jagged shoreline — longer than the California coast. If Maine's coastline is measured in a straight line, however, it is only 228 miles (364 kilometers) long. The salt air of the coast gives way to the scent of pine as one travels inland. Forests cover much of the state. Rivers such as the Penobscot slice through these woods as they flow toward the Atlantic Ocean.

Nature's Bounty

Many "Mainers" depend on the sea for their living. Maine's lobster catch is the largest of any state, supplying about half of the country's lobsters. Thanks to its huge forests, Maine is a major producer of lumber, paper, and other wood products — from baseball bats to toothpicks. Potatoes are another important part of Maine's economy. Grown in the northern part of the state, potatoes account for nearly 30 percent of Maine's agricultural income. Maine is also the largest producer of blueberries in the United States.

Boats and lobster crates are part of the scenery in Bar Harbor, which has long been a favorite resort area.

Timeline

1607
English settlers establish Popham Colony

1631
First Maine sawmill begins production; lumber is exported

1636
Maine's first government established by Ferdinando Gorges

1677
Massachusetts purchases Maine from Gorges family

1794
Bowdoin College opens

1809
Brunswick is site of early textile mills

1820
Maine becomes 23rd state

1842
Treaty settles dispute over Maine/Canada border

Soviet youths greet Samantha Smith in 1983 at the airport.

Samantha Smith

In 1982, during what was called the Cold War, a young Maine girl wrote a letter to Soviet Premier Yuri Andropov encouraging peace between the United States and what was then the Soviet Union (present-day Russia and other nearby countries). Her letter was so effective that she was asked to visit the Soviet Union as an ambassador for peace. Sadly, Samantha and her father died in a 1985 plane crash, but her accomplishments and dreams are not forgotten. A statue of Samantha stands outside the Maine State Museum, and a mountain in Russia is named for her.

Men bring supplies by boat to an isolated lighthouse.

The Way It Was . . . Life in a Lighthouse

Nearly 65 lighthouses dot the Maine coast. Some of them have guided sailors for more than 200 years. The oldest of the lighthouses, Portland Head Light, was built in 1787 by order of George Washington. Today lighthouses are automated, but in the 1700s and 1800s a lighthouse keeper and his or her family lived and worked inside the lighthouse. Oil lamps had to be kept burning all night long to help sailors avoid crashing into the rocky shore. Perched on high places, the lighthouses were unprotected from severe weather. During violent storms, the keeper's job was very dangerous. Tales of heroism during bad weather have been passed down from one generation to the next. For example, one lighthouse keeper rang a bell for 20 hours during heavy fog to warn ships of the rocky coast before them.

Maine's state animal is the moose. It is the largest antlered animal in North America.

State Facts

Maine Flag

Chickadee

White Pine Cone and Tassel

White Pine

Nickname
Pine Tree State

Capital
Augusta

Area
30,862 square miles
(79,932 sq km)
Rank: 39th

Population
1,317,300
Rank: 40th

Statehood
March 15, 1820
23rd state admitted

Principal Rivers
Kennebec River,
Penobscot River

Highest Point
Mount Katahdin,
5,267 feet (1,605 m)

Motto
Dirigo
(I direct)

Song
"State of Maine Song"

Famous People
Stephen King, Henry Wadsworth Longfellow, Edna St. Vincent Millay, Nelson Rockefeller, Samantha Smith

---

1866
Great Portland fire

1884
Bath Iron Works begins production

1923
Edna St. Vincent Millay wins Pulitzer Prize for poetry

1919
Acadia National Park opens, initially as Lafayette National Park

1969
First state income tax passed in Maine

1948
Margaret Chase Smith becomes first woman elected to U.S. Senate

1998
Severe ice storm causes statewide damage

1980
Settlement of Native American Land Claims

2003
State launches Maine Green Power program

Map labels: CANADA, Madawaska, St. John, Fort Kent, Caribou, CANADA, Presque Isle, Chamberlain Lake, Houlton, Mount Katahdin 5,267 Ft. 1,605 M., Moosehead Lake, Chiputneticook Lakes, MOUNTAINS, APPALACHIAN, KATAHDIN MTS., Millinocket, Kennebec, Penobscot, St. Croix, NEW HAMPSHIRE, Skowhegan, Bangor, Orono, Eastport, Rumford, Waterville, Ellsworth, Bethel, BLUE MTS., Augusta, Bar Harbor, Lewiston, Rockland, ACADIA NAT'L. PK., Auburn, Brunswick, Sebago Lake, Bath, ATLANTIC OCEAN, Portland, Biddeford, Kennebunk, Kittery, Portsmouth, © Rand McNally N-CUS26000-P1- -1 -1 -1

MARYLAND

The English colony—and later, the state—Maryland was named in honor of Henrietta Maria, wife of England's King Charles I. Maryland's nickname, the "Old Line State," was earned during the Revolutionary War. Maryland soldiers "held the line" against the British to ensure safety for General George Washington and his troops at the Battle of Long Island. Of the 404 Maryland soldiers who fought in that battle, 308 died.

Chesapeake Bay

Chesapeake Bay, the largest bay in the United States, lies mostly in Maryland. The huge bay divides the state into two parts, the Eastern Shore and the Western Shore. With a maximum depth of 190 feet (58 meters), the bay is deep enough for ocean liners to travel to Annapolis and Baltimore. The name *Chesapeake* comes from a Native American word that means "great shellfish bay." Oysters, clams, and crabs all flourish here. Commercial fishers and people who enjoy sailing and recreational fishing flock to this popular vacation spot. Maryland crab cakes are only one of the many products that come from the thriving fishing industry in Chesapeake Bay.

Baltimore's Inner Harbor

"The Star-Spangled Banner"

Fierce fighting at Baltimore's Fort McHenry during the War of 1812 inspired Francis Scott Key to pen what was to become the United States' national anthem. Having burned parts of Washington, D.C., the British attacked Baltimore. Key was on a British ship in Chesapeake Bay, trying to negotiate a captive friend's release. The battle raged through the night, but when the sun rose, Key saw that the American flag still flew. Inspired by the sight, Key wrote the first verse of "The Star-Spangled Banner" on a scrap of paper. In 1931, Key's song became the national anthem of the United States.

The sun rises over crab boats on Chesapeake Bay.

Graduation Day at the U.S. Naval Academy in Annapolis

Timeline

1632 King Charles I of England grants Maryland charter to George Calvert, 1st Lord Baltimore

1788 Maryland becomes seventh state

1814 Francis Scott Key writes "The Star Spangled Banner"

1837 The *Baltimore Sun* newspaper establish[ed]

1608 Captain John Smith explores Chesapeake Bay

1694 Capital moved to Annapolis

1791 Maryland gives land for District of Columbia

1829 The Chesapeake and Delaware Canal opens

1845 U.S. Naval Academy foun[ded] in Annapolis

State Facts

Maryland Flag

Baltimore Oriole

Black-Eyed Susan

White Oak

Harriet Tubman

The Way It Was . . . Harriet Tubman and the Underground Railroad

Harriet Tubman was born a slave on a plantation in Maryland around 1820. In 1849, she escaped. Before the Civil War, Tubman secretly went deep into the South to help other slaves escape to the North by means of the Underground Railroad. She made this dangerous journey 19 times. The Underground Railroad was not an actual railway, but rather a secret system of hiding places and people who helped runaway slaves escape to northern states or to Canada. Tubman helped about 300 people escape and was never caught.

Swimming Ponies

Hundreds of years ago, a ship carrying horses and ponies crashed and sank near Assateague Island. Some of the ponies survived, and their descendants now run wild and free on the island. For most of each year, the ponies graze in the marshes of Assateague Island National Seashore, which is shared by Maryland and Virginia. Every summer, the ponies swim to nearby Chincoteague Island. This annual pony drive draws many tourists and also inspired the classic children's novel *Misty of Chincoteague* by Marguerite Henry.

A wild mare and her colt splash through the shallows on Assateague Island.

Nickname
Old Line State

Capital
Annapolis

Area
9,774 square miles
(25,315 sq km)
Rank: 42nd

Population
5,558,100
Rank: 19th

Statehood
April 28, 1788
7th state admitted

Principal Rivers
Patuxent River,
Potomac River

Highest Point
Backbone Mountain,
3,360 feet (1,024 m)

Motto
Fatti maschii, parole femine (Manly deeds, womanly words)

Song
"Maryland, My Maryland"

Famous People
Spiro Agnew,
Billie Holiday,
Francis Scott Key,
George Herman "Babe"
Ruth, Harriet Tubman

1904
Fire destroys much of Baltimore

1952
Chesapeake Bay Bridge completed

1977
Francis Scott Key Bridge opens

1982
Program developed to improve water quality in Chesapeake Bay

2001
Baltimore Ravens win their first Super Bowl

1967
Thurgood Marshall becomes first African American U.S. Supreme Court justice

1981
National Aquarium opens in Baltimore

1995
Baltimore Orioles' Cal Ripken breaks Lou Gehrig's record of playing in 2,130 consecutive baseball games

MASSACHUSETTS

A statue of Paul Revere in front of the Old North Church recalls his famous ride.

Massachusetts has a rich history and is home to many firsts in the United States. In the 1760s and 1770s, Massachusetts colonists helped lead the struggle for independence from Britain. The first battles of the Revolutionary War took place at Lexington and Concord. Massachusetts also took the lead in another revolution — the Industrial Revolution. Some of the first American textile mills, shoe factories, and iron works were located in Massachusetts. Harvard, the first college in the United States, was founded in Cambridge. The state itself takes its name from people who were there first — the Massachusett, a Native American tribe.

The Freedom Trail

The past is a vital part of modern Massachusetts. In Boston, especially, history has left many traces. Gleaming skyscrapers rise above red-brick buildings that are more than 200 years old. Red lines on the sidewalks mark the Freedom Trail, which leads to many historic sites. Those landmarks include Paul Revere's house, the Old North Church, the site of the Boston Massacre, and the Old South Meeting House, where patriots gathered to march to Griffin's Wharf for the Boston Tea Party.

Tourism in Massachusetts

Tourism is an important industry in a state with so much to see and do. Along the coast are many charming old fishing villages. Many tourists visit Salem to see where the notorious witch trials took place in 1692. World-famous colleges and universities, such as Harvard University and the Massachusetts Institute of Technology, draw tourists as well as scholars to their grounds. Massachusetts also is home to sandy beaches like those on Cape Cod, which juts out into the Atlantic Ocean.

Colorful boats along the shore of Cape Cod

Timeline

1498
John Cabot explores the Massachusetts coast

1620
Pilgrims found Plymouth

1630
Boston founded

1636
Harvard, first college in U.S., established

1639
First U.S. post office established in Boston

1675-1676
King Philip's War between colonists and Native Americans

1770
Boston Massacre

1773
Boston Tea Party

1775
Battles at Lexington and Concord mark beginning of Revolutionary War

Map Labels

VERMONT

NEW HAMPSHIRE

NEW YORK

North Adams

+ Mt. Greylock 3,487 Ft. 1,063 M.

Greenfield

Athol

Fitchburg

Haverhill

Lawrence

Lowell

Merrimack

Gloucester

Gardner

Leominster

Salem

BERKSHIRE HILLS

Pittsfield

Amherst

Quabbin Reservoir

+ Wachusett Mtn. 2006 Ft. 611 M.

Concord

Lexington

Concord

Cambridge

Boston

Massachusetts Bay

Boston Bay

Northampton

Worcester

Framingham

ATLANTIC OCEAN

Housatonic

Holyoke

Chicopee

Charles

Springfield

Southbridge

CONNECTICUT

RHODE ISLAND

Brockton

Provincetown

CAPE COD NAT'L. SEASHORE

Attleboro

Plymouth

Taunton

Cape Cod Bay

CAPE COD

Fall River

Hyannis

New Bedford

Buzzards Bay

Nantucket Sound

ELIZABETH ISLANDS

MARTHA'S VINEYARD

NANTUCKET ISLAND

© Rand McNally
N-CUS26200-P1- -1-1-1

0   10 Mi.
0   10 Km.

Literary Massachusetts

Two of the most important authors of the 19th century, Emily Dickinson and Nathaniel Hawthorne, were from Massachusetts. Dickinson was a reclusive resident of Amherst who produced poems of great power and insight. Her fame came when her poems were published after her death in 1886. Hawthorne's most famous novel is *The Scarlet Letter*. In Salem, tourists can visit Hawthorne's birthplace and the house that served as the inspiration for his novel *The House of the Seven Gables*.

Built in 1813, the Dickinson homestead in Amherst is a favorite destination of students and tourists.

A Pilgrim woman shares the feast with Native Americans.

The Way It Was . . . The First Thanksgiving

In December 1620, a group of English colonists sailing on the *Mayflower* arrived in what is now Massachusetts. The colonists, later known as the Pilgrims, built a settlement they called Plymouth. That first winter at Plymouth was harsh; about half the colonists died of starvation and disease. The following spring, a Native American named Samoset greeted the Pilgrims. He introduced them to Squanto and Massasoit, leaders of the Wampanoag tribe. The Native Americans taught the Pilgrims how to plant corn and where to fish and hunt. That fall, the Pilgrims had a fine harvest. They invited the Native Americans to celebrate the harvest and their friendship. This was the start of the Thanksgiving holiday that Americans celebrate each November.

Timeline

1788
Massachusetts becomes 6th state

1903
Baseball's first World Series held in Boston

1991
Boston Harbor clean-up begins

2004
Red Sox sweep World Series

1897
First subway in U.S. opens in Boston

1960
Massachusetts native John F. Kennedy elected president of the U.S.

2003
Boston's "Big Dig" tunnel opens to traffic

MICHIGAN

The name *Michigan* comes from a Native American phrase, *michi gami*, which means "great lake." The name certainly fits this midwestern state, because Michigan is bordered by four of the five Great Lakes. Long ago, the trade of wolves' fur was important to the growing territory of Michigan. Today, tourism, agriculture, and manufacturing are leading economic activities. Michigan's lakes, forests, and beaches attract millions of visitors each year.

Factory workers assemble Ford cars in 1930.

Two Different Peninsulas

Michigan consists of two separate land areas — the Upper Peninsula and the Lower Peninsula — which are connected by a five-mile (eight-kilometer) bridge across the Straits of Mackinac. Together the two peninsulas have more than 3,000 miles (4,800 kilometers) of shoreline. The Upper Peninsula, sometimes called the "U.P.," has a colder climate than that of the Lower Peninsula.

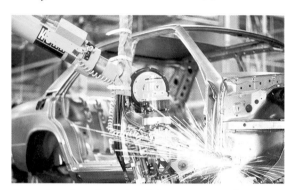
In modern factories, robots help put cars together.

Mackinac Island is one of Michigan's most popular tourist destinations.

The Motor City

Detroit, Michigan's largest city, is also known as "Motor City." A great majority of the cars manufactured in the United States are made in the Detroit area. Detroit's automobile industry got its start when Ransom E. Olds founded the Olds Motor Works in 1899. Henry Ford, who started the Ford Motor Company in 1903, introduced the moving assembly line. This method helped save time and money. With today's technology, cars can be assembled in about an hour — a fraction of the time it took in Ford's day.

Timeline

1620
Étienne Brulé explores Upper Peninsula

1668
First permanent settlement, Sault Ste. Marie, founded

1701
Detroit established

1760
British take control of land from French

1783
Revolutionary War leaves U.S. in control of land

1805
Territory of Michigan established

1812
British seize Fort Mackinac and Detroit

1837
Michigan becomes 26th state

ISLE ROYALE NAT'L. PARK
LAKE SUPERIOR
0 10 Mi.
0 10 Km.

KEWEENAW PENINSULA

0 15 30 Mi.
0 20 40 Km.

COPPER RANGE

LAKE SUPERIOR

CANADA

Ironwood

Mt. Arvon + 1,979 Ft. 603 M.

Marquette

Ishpeming

Sault Ste. Marie

DRUMMOND ISLAND

Manistique

Iron Mtn.

WISCONSIN

Straits of Mackinac

MACKINAC I.

BOIS BLANC I.

Mackinaw City

BEAVER ISLAND

Menominee

WASHINGTON I.

NORTH MANITOU I.

SOUTH MANITOU I.

Green Bay

Petoskey

Grand Traverse Bay

Alpena

Thunder Bay

LAKE HURON

Traverse City

Manistee

Grayling

LAKE MICHIGAN

Manistee

Cadillac

Ludington

Muskegon

Saginaw

Saginaw Bay

Muskegon

Grand Rapids

Flint

Port Huron

Lake St. Clair

CANADA

⭐ Lansing

Holland

Warren

Livonia

Dearborn

Detroit

Kalamazoo

Jackson

Kalamazoo

Battle Creek

Ann Arbor

Windsor

Benton Harbor

Monroe

INDIANA

OHIO

Toledo

LAKE ERIE

© Rand McNally
N-CUS26300-P1- -1-1-1

Mackinac Island

Mackinac Island is a well-known resort island located between Michigan's Upper and Lower Peninsulas. The only way to reach the island is by boat. Once visitors arrive, they must either walk or bike to get around the island — no passenger cars are allowed. The absence of cars helps create a quiet, relaxed atmosphere. Besides boating and biking, most visitors browse in tiny shops and munch on the famous Michigan fudge sold by vendors.

Dr. John Kellogg, director of health resorts in Michigan and Florida

The Way It Was . . .
The Capital of Corn Flakes

Battle Creek produces more breakfast cereal than any other city in the world. In the late 1800s, Dr. John Kellogg of Battle Creek experimented with special diets that he hoped would help his patients. One of his experiments led to a new food product: baked wheat flakes. In 1906, Dr. Kellogg's younger brother, W. K. Kellogg, introduced corn flakes. That same year, C.W. Post invented and marketed his own version of corn flakes. Today, visitors to Battle Creek can tour the cereal factories and sample some of the many breakfast foods made there.

Settled by Dutch immigrants in 1847, the town of Holland is known for tulips and wooden shoes.

State Facts

Michigan Flag

Robin

Apple Blossom

White Pine

Nickname
Wolverine State

Capital
Lansing

Area
56,804 square miles
(147,122 sq km)
Rank: 22nd

Population
10,112,600
Rank: 8th

Statehood
January 26, 1837
26th state admitted

Principal River
Muskegon River

Highest Point
Mount Arvon,
1,979 feet (603 m)

Motto
Si quaeris peninsulam amoenam circumspice
(If you seek a pleasant peninsula, look about you)

Song
"Michigan, My Michigan"

Famous People
Henry Ford, John Kellogg,
W. K. Kellogg,
Earvin "Magic" Johnson,
Charles Lindbergh,
Diana Ross

1854
Republican Party formally adopts its name at Jackson

1894
First wheat flakes made by Kellogg brothers

1930
Detroit-Windsor tunnel opens

1991
Michigan Scenic Rivers Act is passed

1847
Lansing becomes state capital

1855
Soo Locks connect Lake Huron and Lake Superior

1899
Ransom E. Olds opens Michigan's first automobile factory

1957
Mackinac Bridge completed

2002
Jennifer Granholm becomes state's first woman governor

MINNESOTA

The name *Minnesota* comes from a Sioux phrase meaning "sky-colored waters." Minnesota has more than 10,000 clear blue lakes, most of which are found in the the northern half of the state. Although beautiful, Minnesota can be hot in the summer and extremely cold in the winter. International Falls, at the Canadian border, is sometimes called the "nation's ice-box." There, temperatures of 20° Fahrenheit (-29° Celsius) are common in winter.

The Twin Cities

Half of Minnesota's population lives in the Twin Cities of Minneapolis and St. Paul. Are these cities really "twins"? They aren't identical, but both are large cities, one on each side of the Mississippi River. Minneapolis is the largest city in the state, and St. Paul, the second largest, is the state's capital. The Twin Cities have many skyscrapers, some with enclosed walkways betweem them. In the cold winter, busy workers and shoppers need not go out-side to get from building to building. Nearby Bloom-ington is the third largest city in the state and home to the Mall of America, the largest shopping mall in the United States. In addition to about 400 stores, the mall has its own amusement park and aquarium.

A canoe floats on the tranquil water of Lake Itasca.

Icicles on a bicycle during one of Minnesota's harsh winters

Lake Itasca State Park

The mighty Mississippi River begins in Minnesota at Lake Itasca. The great river — one of the longest in the world — begins in Lake Itasca State Park as a small stream that is only about ten feet (three meters) wide and two feet (.6 meters) deep. The state park is home to a herd of buffalo, one of the few herds left in the United States. Red foxes, moose, beavers, and wolves also live in the park. Visitors enjoy the sparkling water, clean air, and beautiful scenery from their campsites and canoes. They may also hear the haunting cry of the state bird, the common loon.

Timeline

1679
Daniel Greysolon, Sieur Duluth, explores Minnesota

1689
Nicholas Perrot builds fort on Lake Pepin

1763
Britain wins eastern Minnesota from France

1783
Treaty of Paris gives part of Minnesota to U.S.

1803
All of Minnesota becomes part of U.S.

1832
Henry Schoolcraft discovers Lake Itasca as source of Mississippi River

1849
Congress creates Minnesota Territory

1852
Minneapolis established

1858
Minnesota become 32nd state

Lumberjack Lore

The tall tales of the giant lumberjack Paul Bunyan and his blue ox, Babe, were first relayed in lumber camps many years ago. According to these stories, Bunyan formed the Mississippi River when he tipped over the tub in which he was doing laundry. The stories also claim that Bunyan and Babe made Minnesota's many lakes when their giant footprints filled with rainwater and melting snow. Statues of Bunyan and Babe can be seen near the towns of Bemidji and Brainerd.

Swedish settlers in Boston prepare for the long journey to Minnesota.

The Way It Was . . . Coming to America

Minnesota has a large population of Scandinavians — that is, people whose ancestors lived in Sweden, Denmark, Norway, or Finland. In the 1850s, Scandinavians who had settled in Minnesota wrote letters praising America to friends and family members back home. These letters were copied, passed around, and even published in newspapers. As a result, many other Scandinavians — sometimes entire villages — left their homelands, where land and food were scarce, to come to the United States. By 1860, the railroads had reached Minnesota, making travel from the eastern United States easier for those who wanted to join the thousands of Scandinavians already living in Minnesota. Norway and Sweden tried to stop their citizens from moving to Minnesota, but the lure of the American dream proved too strong.

In winter, many Minnesota lakes freeze over. This young boy patiently awaits a tug on his fishing line as the sun begins to set.

State Facts

Minnesota Flag

Common Loon

Pink-and-white Lady's Slipper

Norway Pine

Nickname
North Star State

Capital
St. Paul

Area
79,610 square miles
(206,189 sq km)
Rank: 14th

Population
5,101,000
Rank: 21st

Statehood
May 11, 1858
32nd state admitted

Principal Rivers
Mississipi River, Red River

Highest Point
Eagle Mountain,
2,301 feet (701 m)

Motto
L'Etoile du nord
(The north star)

Song
"Hail! Minnesota"

Famous People
Bob Dylan,
F. Scott Fitzgerald,
Garrison Keillor,
Sinclair Lewis,
Roger Maris

1868
Grange movement for farmers starts

1889
Mayo Clinic founded in Rochester

1890
Iron ore discovered in Mesabi Range

1894
Fire destroys towns of Hinckley and Sandstone

1905
State capitol construction completed

1930
Sinclair Lewis wins Nobel Prize for literature

1991
Minnesota Twins win World Series

1992
Mall of America opens

1999
Native Americans successfully sue state for more hunting and fishing rights

MISSISSIPPI

An old-fashioned paddle wheeler churns its way down the Mississippi River.

Vicksburg National Military Park commemorates a great Civil War battle fought in 1863.

The Lay of the Land

Mississippi is a land of plains and low hills. Farmers of the fertile Yazoo Basin raise bumper crops of corn and soybeans. Farther south, the Pine Hills — often called the Piney Woods — yield lumber and other forest products. Mississippi's coast along the Gulf of Mexico is a popular vacation area due to its warm climate and pleasant beaches. The Black Prairie in northeastern Mississippi is named for its rich, dark soil, which is excellent for growing grass for hay and other crops.

The southern state of Mississippi is named after the river that forms its western border. The river's name means "father of the waters" in the language spoken by Native Americans who once lived in the upper Mississippi Valley. Mississippi's weather is warm and moist year-round. The climate is perfect for growing magnolias and crops such as cotton, which until the 1930s was the mainstay of Mississippi's economy. Since then, factories that produce electrical and transportation goods have become important, too.

The Mighty Mississippi

The Mississippi River is the second-longest river in the United States, stretching 2,348 miles (3,757 kilometers). An important pathway for people and goods, the river forms borders of nine states besides Mississippi. Floods caused by lots of rain and melting snow can occur along the Mississippi. Walls called levees have been built along the river's banks to help hold back rising waters and thus prevent flood damage.

Stanton Hall is located in the heart of Natchez. Frederick Stanton built the elegant home in 1857.

Timeline

1540
Hernando de Soto explores Mississippi

1699
First French colony established at Old Biloxi

1763
English take control of Mississippi

1798
Mississippi Territory established

1799
The *Mississippi Gazette* first published

1817
Mississippi becomes 20th state

1844
University of Mississippi opens

1863
Union forces capture Vicksburg

Cotton Was King

In 1540, Spanish explorers brought the first cottonseeds to what is now Mississippi. As a result, cotton became the staple of the area's economy. "King Cotton" reigned for many years. The 1939 discovery of oil in Mississippi helped the state industrialize. Today, Mississippi factories produce a wide variety of goods, from foods to ships to stereo equipment.

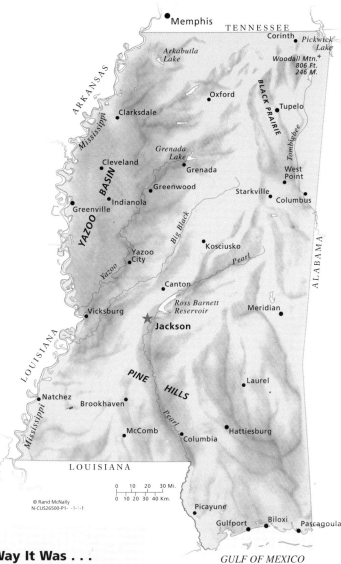

Memphis
TENNESSEE
Corinth
Pickwick Lake
Arkabutla Lake
Woodall Mtn. + 806 Ft. 246 M.
Oxford
BLACK PRAIRIE
Clarksdale
Tupelo
Mississippi
YAZOO BASIN
Grenada Lake
Cleveland
Grenada
West Point
Greenwood
Starkville
Columbus
Indianola
Greenville
ALABAMA
Big Black
Yazoo
Kosciusko
Yazoo City
Pearl
Canton
Ross Barnett Reservoir
Meridian
Vicksburg
LOUISIANA
★ Jackson
PINE HILLS
Laurel
Natchez
Brookhaven
Pearl
Hattiesburg
McComb
Columbia
LOUISIANA

0 10 20 30 Mi.
0 10 20 30 40 Km.
© Rand McNally
N-CUS26500-P1- -1-1-1

Picayune
Gulfport
Biloxi
Pascagoula

GULF OF MEXICO

Residents struggled with water in their homes and driveways.

The Way It Was . . . Mississippi Mud Pie

In 1927, a raging flood hit the town of Greenville, which remained under water for seventy days. When the water finally went down, Mississippi mud was all that remained. Two years later, Chef Percy Tolliver developed a frozen pie with a chocolate cookie crust, ice cream filling, and a fudge sauce topping. One hot and humid summer day, a server at Tolliver's restaurant rushed to get a piece of the pie to a customer before it completely melted. The customer looked at the oozing pie and said, "That reminds me of that Mississippi mud." From then on, Tolliver's concoction — a popular dessert in Mississippi and elsewhere — had a name.

Shrimp boats line the docks along Mississippi's Gulf Coast.

1927
Mississippi River flood leaves thousands homeless

1939
Oil discovered at Tinsley

1969
Hurricane Camille strikes coastline

1990
Gambling legalized

1936
Balance Agriculture with Industry (BAWI) program adopted

1949
William Faulkner receives Nobel Prize for literature

1985
Tombigbee Waterway completed

2002
Mississippi becomes first state with internet access in every classroom

MISSOURI

The Gateway Arch in St. Louis

Missouri is named for the Missouri River, the longest river in the United States, which flows through its center. The river got its name from a Native American word that means "muddy water" or "town of the large canoes." The Mississippi River flows along Missouri's eastern edge. The state shares borders with eight other states. Its central location and two great rivers have made it a major transportation center.

Geography

Missouri has two distinct regions. The area north of the Missouri River is mostly flat with a few rolling hills. Corn, wheat, and soybeans all grow well there. South of the Missouri River, the Ozark Plateau is a mountainous area with many caves and natural springs. The Missouri and the Mississippi Rivers meet near St. Louis. In the 1800s, pioneers often made Missouri a stopping point on their westward journey. The Pony Express, which once delivered mail throughout the West, was started in Missouri in 1860.

Built in 1894, Alley Roller Mill is an Ozark landmark.

Branson has become famous for its live music theaters. Thousands of people visit every year to attend shows.

The Ozarks

Southern Missouri's Ozark Mountains are a popular vacation area. The mountains are filled with natural springs and scenic rivers, some of which have been dammed, creating wonderful lakes where visitors can fish and swim. Explorers also can enjoy the thousands of caves that have been discovered in these mountains. Elephant Rocks State Park has many large, unique rock formations. One of the largest rocks, nicknamed "Dumbo," weighs 680 tons (612 metric tons).

Timeline

1682
René-Robert Cavelier, Sieur de La Salle, claims Missouri for France

1750
First permanent settlement established at Ste. Genevieve

1762
France cedes territory to Spain

1764
St. Louis founded

1800
France regains territory from Spain

1803
Missouri becomes part of the U.S. through Louisiana Purchase

1808
First Missouri newspaper, the *Missouri Gazette*, published

1811-1812
Three largest earthquakes in American history strike near New Madrid

© Rand McNally
N-CUS26600-P1- -1-1-1

*Samuel Clemens,
known as Mark
Twain to readers*

Mark Twain

Mark Twain, whose real name
was Samuel Clemens, is the
author of the famous books
The Adventures of Tom Sawyer
and *The Adventures of
Huckleberry Finn.* Twain was
born in a log cabin in 1835 and
grew up in Hannibal. The house
in which he grew up looks
much like the fictional Tom
Sawyer's house, including a
white picket fence. Today
visitors can tour Twain's house
as well as other Missouri sites
that Twain featured in his
many writings.

*The nearly completed
Gateway Arch*

The Way It Was . . . The Gateway Arch

In 1934, a group of St. Louis citizens
decided that a monument to honor
St. Louis's role in the settlement of
the West should be built. They did
not carry out those plans until 1947,
when a design contest was held. The judges sifted through 172 entries
before choosing one submitted by the architect Eero Saarinen, whose
father also had entered the contest. Construction of the Gateway Arch
was finally finished in 1965. The Arch, which symbolizes St. Louis's
role as the Gateway to the West, is now a top tourist attraction in
the city. Visitors can travel in small trains through the hollow arch.
At the top, they can peer out tiny windows to view St. Louis and the
surrounding countryside below.

1821
Missouri becomes
24th state

1904
Louisiana Purchase
Exposition held at St. Louis

1965
Construction completed on
Gateway Arch in St. Louis

1993
Major floods hit
Missouri

1812
Missouri Territory
created by Congress

1859
Railroad service in
Missouri begins

1945
Harry S Truman
becomes 33rd
president of the U.S.

1985
Kansas City Royals
win World Series

2004
Matt Blunt is elected gov-
ernor, one of youngest in
U.S. at time of his election

MONTANA

With miles and miles of jagged, snowy peaks, Montana lives up to its name, which comes from the Spanish word for "mountain." However, the majestic Rocky Mountains of western Montana are just part of the state's geographic story. The rest of Montana lies within the Great Plains, a huge region of flat or gently rolling land. Viewed from Montana's plains, the sky seems especially vast, which is why residents of Montana call their home Big Sky Country.

Mountains and Plains

In eastern Montana, wheat fields and cattle ranches, dotted by an occasional farmhouse, sprawl across the plains. In western Montana, broad, grassy valleys separate the forested mountain ranges that make up the Rockies. Glacier National Park lies in this region. The park is named for the more than 50 glaciers found there. Some of the mountains in the park are so icy and steep that they have never been climbed. The park is just one of many features that attract hikers, campers, and other visitors to Montana.

Formed over the last few thousand years, the young glaciers in Glacier National Park are slowly melting.

Mineral Wealth

Montana is sometimes called the Treasure State because of its rich mineral resources. The discovery of gold in 1862 attracted droves of prospectors. Some of the boom towns that sprang up, such as Helena, survived and even thrived. Others became ghost towns after "gold fever" died down. Today, Montanans still mine gold, as well as silver, copper, lead, and other metals. Central Montana is the only spot in the United States where sapphires are mined. The state's most important resources, though, are coal and oil.

Weathered front of an abandoned building in a Montana ghost town

Bison roam the fertile Montana plains.

Timeline

1743
Francois and Louis-Joseph la Verendrye explore Montana

1803
Most of Montana acquired by U.S. through Louisiana Purchase

1805
Meriwether Lewis and William Clark explore Montana

1847
Fort Benton established

1862
John White discovers gold in southwestern Montana

1864
Montana territory created

1875
Helena becomes capital

1876
Custer defeated at Battle of the Little Bighorn

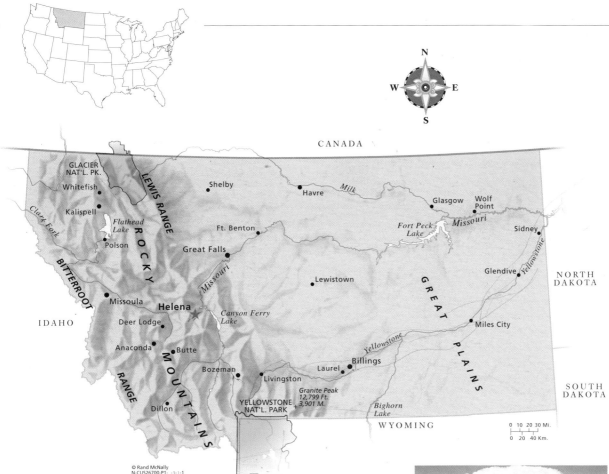

© Rand McNally
N-CUS26700-P1- -1-1-1

State Facts

Montana Flag

Western Meadowlark

Bitterroot

Ponderosa Pine

Nickname
Treasure State

Capital
Helena

Area
145,552 square miles
(376,978 sq km)
Rank: 4th

Population
926,900
Rank: 44th

Statehood
November 8, 1889
41st state admitted

Principal Rivers
Missouri River,
Yellowstone River

Highest Point
Granite Peak,
12,799 feet (3,901 m)

Motto
Oro y plata
(Gold and silver)

Song
"Montana"

Famous People
Gary Cooper,
Grace Eldering,
Jeannette Rankin

Montana's sweeping grasslands are well suited to ranching.

The Way It Was . . . Custer's Last Stand

As miners and other settlers poured into Montana and nearby areas in the mid-1800s, bloody conflicts erupted between them and the Native Americans who lived and hunted in the region. The United States government sent soldiers to defend the settlers and "subdue" the Indians. One of the most famous battles between the army and Native Americans occurred on June 25, 1876, near the Little Bighorn River in southeastern Montana. There about 210 soldiers led by Lieutenant Colonel George A. Custer fought a much larger force of Cheyenne and Sioux led by Crazy Horse. Every one of the U.S. soldiers, including Custer, was killed in what became known as "Custer's Last Stand."

None of the United States soldiers lived to describe the Battle of Little Bighorn.

Montana Wildlife

Montana teems with wildlife. Its wild land animals include elk, mountain goats, mountain sheep, moose, grizzly bears, and antelopes. Birds include trumpeter swans and bald eagles. Lakes and streams abound with cutthroat trout and grayling. Montana also has large populations of livestock. Vast herds of cattle and sheep graze on the plains. Horses make their appearance on working ranches, on dude ranches, and in rodeos.

1877
Chief Joseph and the Nez Percé Indians surrender

1889
Montana becomes 41st state

1893
University of Montana established in Missoula

1910
Congress creates Glacier National Park

100 YEARS

1973
New state constitution goes into effect

1989
Montana celebrates its centennial

2000
Severe wildfires spread across state

NEBRASKA

The Great Plains state of Nebraska is mostly a land of farms. It has only two major cities: Omaha and Lincoln. Smaller towns dot the state's seemingly endless miles of fields and prairies. The name *Nebraska* comes from the Oto word *nebrathka*, which means "flat water." The flat water in Nebraska is the wide but very shallow Platte River. Nebraska is also known as the Cornhusker State. Long ago, people in Nebraska held cornhusking parties. These gatherings gave farm families a chance to visit while they removed the husks from the ears of corn they had grown.

Chimney Rock, a well-known landmark along the Oregon Trail

Geography

Eastern Nebraska is a rolling land covered with rich soil left by melting glaciers thousands of years ago. Further west, the land becomes drier and rougher. The Sand Hills region is the largest area of sand dunes in North America. In the far western part of the state, a large rock formation, Chimney Rock, juts above the sandy landscape. Visible from over 30 miles (48 kilometers) away, Chimney Rock guided many early pioneers on their journey west.

Farms and Ranches

Nearly 95 percent of Nebraska is farmland and grazing land. The fertile soil in the east is excellent for crops such as corn and soybeans. In southern Nebraska, farmers grow wheat. Ranches are found across the state, particularly in the west. The grasses of the Sand Hills region provide food for beef cattle. Nearly six million cattle and calves are raised in Nebraska every year. In addition, hog farms and turkey farms can be found in the state.

Rodeos are a popular way to showcase ranching skills.

Cattle graze in a lush farm pasture.

Timeline

1793
Pierre and Paul Mallet explore Nebraska

1803
U.S. acquires Nebraska through Louisiana Purchase

1804
Meriwether Lewis and William Clark explore Nebraska

1819
Fort Atkinson established

1823
First permanent white settlement established at Bellevue

1854
Kansas-Nebraska Act opens region to settlement

1867
Nebraska becomes 37th state

1875
Present state constitution adopted

1877
Sioux leader Crazy Horse surrenders to U.S. Army

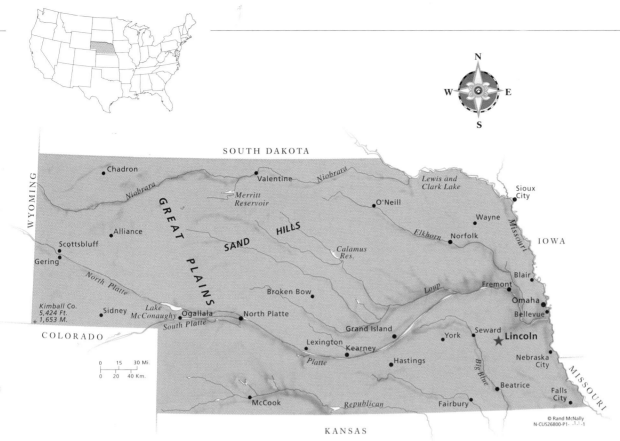

© Rand McNally
N-CUS26800-P1-

State Facts

Nebraska Flag

Western Meadowlark

Goldenrod

Cottonwood

Nickname
Cornhusker State

Capital
Lincoln

Area
76,872 square miles
(199,098 sq km)
Rank: 15th

Population
1,747,200
Rank: 38th

Statehood
March 1, 1867
37th state admitted

Principal Rivers
Missouri River,
Platte River

Highest Point
5,424 feet (1,653 m),
in Kimball County

Motto
Equality before the law

Song
"Beautiful Nebraska"

Famous People
Fred Astaire,
Marlon Brando,
William "Buffalo Bill" Cody,
Henry Fonda,
Gerald R. Ford, Ted Kooser,
Malcolm X

Soddies

The Homestead Act of 1862 offered 160 acres (64 hectares) of land to people who agreed to live on the land for five years and improve it. In response, thousands of homesteaders came to Nebraska and other Great Plains areas. With few trees to cut down for houses, they used sod — the top layer of grass and soil that covered their land. They cut the sod into blocks, stacked them, and packed mud between them to hold them together. The houses they made were called soddies. The houses were very sturdy; in fact, some soddies are still standing today.

Sturdy soddy on the prairie

The Way It Was . . . Arbor Day

After settlers used the top layer of grass and soil to build their sod houses, the ground that was left was dry and loose. Wind could blow the soil away and make the land useless for raising crops and grazing livestock. J. Sterling Morton, a Nebraska newspaper publisher, came up with the idea of a tree-planting holiday called Arbor Day. Not only would the trees help keep the soil in place, they would also beautify the landscape. Other Nebraskans were enthusiastic, and by some estimates, more than one million trees were planted that first Arbor Day. The tradition of planting trees on a certain day continues and has spread to many other states.

The first Arbor Day was April 10, 1872.

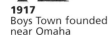

1893
First Cowboy
Horse Race held

1917
Boys Town founded
near Omaha

1932
State Capitol
completed

1939
Oil discovered
near Falls City

1942
Kingsley Dam
completed

1974
Gerald R. Ford becomes
38th president

1982
Initiative 300 prevents large corporations from buying family farms

1997
Cowboy Recreation and
Nature Trail opens

2004
Ted Kooser named U.S.
poet laureate

NEVADA

The Hoover Dam, near Boulder City, generates hydroelectric power for parts of Nevada, Arizona, and California.

Plants and Animals

Nevada is sometimes called the "Sagebrush State," and for good reason. This attractive shrub, with gray-green leaves and white or yellow flowers, dots Nevada's deserts. Other desert plants include cactus, yucca, and mesquite. Despite its dryness, Nevada is home to more than 40 species of fish, including the rare cui-ui, which lives only in Pyramid Lake. Nevada's mountain animals include bighorn sheep and mule deer. Desert animals include several kinds of snakes and lizards.

Bristlecone pines like this one in Great Basin National Park can live to be thousands of years old.

Nevada is one of the warmest states and receives less rain or snow than any other. Because of that, it may seem odd that the state's name comes from a Spanish word meaning "snow-covered." However, Nevada has more than 150 mountain ranges, and many peaks are indeed capped with winter snow. Most of Nevada is thinly populated. In a given year, visitors to places such as Las Vegas and Lake Tahoe greatly outnumber state residents. However, a sunny climate and expanding job opportunities have helped make Nevada's population the fastest growing in the United States.

Land and Water

Nevada's rugged mountain ranges and the valleys that separate them give the state a wrinkled appearance when viewed from high above. Jagged peaks, limestone caves, deep canyons, and red sandstone are just some of the scenic wonders of Nevada's mountain areas. Lake Tahoe lies on the Nevada-California border in a high valley of the Sierra Nevada mountain range. The lake is 6,228 feet (1,887 meters) above sea level. Evergreens line its shores, which also feature public beaches, parks, and resorts.

Lake Tahoe takes its name from a Washo Indian word that means "big water."

Timeline

1821
Nevada becomes part of Mexico

1826
Jedediah Smith is first American to explore Nevada

1848
Nevada becomes part of U.S. after Mexican War

1851
First permanent settlement, Mormon Station, established

1858
Prospectors discover gold and silver near Carson City

1858
Nevada's first newspaper, the Territorial Enterprise, established

1861
Nevada becomes a territory

Sources of Wealth

Tourism is the backbone of Nevada's economy, and Las Vegas is the state's biggest tourist attraction. More than 20 million people visit Las Vegas each year. In addition to gambling casinos and live entertainment, Las Vegas offers fine golf courses and huge theme hotels designed to appeal to entire families. Mining has long been an important part of Nevada's economy, too. As its nickname "Silver State" indicates, Nevada is the country's leading producer of silver.

OREGON   IDAHO

Winnemucca
Humboldt
Wells
Humboldt
Elko
Battle Mountain
RUBY MTS.

Pyramid Lake
GREAT

SIERRA NEVADA
Sparks
Fallon
Reno
Virginia City
Carson City
Lake Tahoe
Yerington
Gardnerville
Walker Lake
Hawthorne

SHOSHONE MTS.
TOIYABE RANGE
MONITOR RANGE
Eureka
Ely
Ely
GREAT BASIN NAT'L. PARK
UTAH

BASIN

CALIFORNIA
Boundary Pk. + 13,140 Ft. 4,005 M.
Tonopah
Pioche

DEATH VALLEY NATIONAL PARK
AMARGOSA DESERT
Las Vegas
Lake Mead
Henderson
Boulder City
Colorado
ARIZONA
Laughlin

0 10 20 30 Mi.
0 20 40 Km.

© Rand McNally
N-CUS26900-P1- .1-.1-.1

Main Street in Virginia City bustles with activity.

The Way It Was . . . Virginia City

In 1858, prospectors working near Carson City made an amazing discovery. While searching for gold, they dug up a sticky soil that was almost pure silver. They had come upon the Comstock Lode, which would prove to be one of the richest mineral finds ever, producing millions of dollars in silver and gold. As news of the find spread, more miners rushed to the site. A new town, Virginia City, sprang up almost overnight. By 1876, when the Comstock mines were at their peak, Virginia City had more than 20,000 people, as well as a railroad, an opera house, and plenty of stores, laundries, and saloons. Many of Nevada's old mining towns are ghost towns today, but Virginia City has been restored and is a popular tourist spot.

Ghost towns across Nevada bear witness to past mining booms.

State Facts

Nevada Flag

Mountain Bluebird

Sagebrush

Single-leaf Pinon

Nickname
Silver State

Capitol
Carson City

Area
109,826 square miles
(284,448 sq km)
Rank: 7th

Population
2,334,800
Rank: 35th

Statehood
October 31, 1864
36th state admitted

Principal Rivers
Colorado River,
Humboldt River

Highest Point
Boundary Peak,
13,140 feet (4,005 m)

Motto
All for our country

Song
"Home Means Nevada"

Famous People
Andre Agassi,
Patricia Ryan Nixon,
Barbara Vucanovich

1864
Nevada becomes 36th state

1875
Virginia City destroyed by fire

1931
Gambling legalized

1951
Nuclear weapons tested in southern Nevada

1996
Fallon becomes home of U. S. Navy's Top Gun flight school

1873
"Big Bonanza" silver lode discovered in Virginia City

1907
Newlands Irrigation Project completed

1936
Hoover Dam on Colorado River completed

1971
Southern Nevada Water Project completed

2000
U.S. Census shows state population more than doubled since 1980

NEW HAMPSHIRE

New Hampshire is known for its magnificent landscapes and year-round outdoor activities. In winter, skiers speed down snowy mountain slopes. In spring and summer, sightseers from elsewhere in New England and beyond enjoy the state's beaches, lakes, and quaint villages. Autumn brings a deluge of visitors to view the trees with their brilliantly colored leaves. New Hampshire, one of the original 13 colonies, takes its name from the county of Hampshire, England, home of founder John Mason.

People and Places

Most residents of New Hampshire live in the south, especially the Merrimack Valley. This area includes the state's three largest cities: Manchester, Nashua, and Concord. The rugged White Mountains region of northern New Hampshire is less populated. The Presidential Range of the White Mountains has the highest peaks in New England. Mount Washington is the tallest of the 86 peaks in the New England range.

The Mt. Washington Cog Railway uses coal-driven steam engines to transport passengers to the mountain's summit.

Autumn leaves blanket the slope leading up to a typical small-town New Hampshire church.

Economy

Manufacturing is the most important industry in New Hampshire. Items manufactured in the state include machinery, computers, scientific instruments, electrical equipment, and paper and other forest products, such as wooden furniture. Tourism is also an important part of New Hampshire's economy. People travel to the state to enjoy its resorts and scenic beauty.

Mt. Washington dwarfs the hotel that shares its name.

Timeline

1603
Martin Pring sails up Piscataqua River

1623
David Thomson and followers settle the region

1630
Strawbery Banke (Portsmouth) is established

1680
New Hampshire becomes a separate royal colony

1686
New Hampshire unites with other colonies to form Dominion of New England

1756
The New Hampshire Gazette established

1769
Dartmouth College founded

1776
New Hampshire is first colony to declare independence from Brita[in]

1788
New Hampshire becomes 9th state

CANADA

Colebrook

Umbagog Lake

MAINE

Berlin

VERMONT

Littleton

Mount Washington 6,288 Ft. + 1,917 M.

WHITE MOUNTAINS

Lebanon

Franklin Falls Res.

Franklin

Lake Winnipesaukee

Laconia

Claremont

Rochester

Dover

★ Concord

Manchester

Portsmouth

Keene

Derry

ATLANTIC OCEAN

Nashua

© Rand McNally
N·CUS27000-P1- -1-1-1

MASSACHUSETTS

0   10 Mi.
0   10 Km.

N
W   E
S

Covered bridges are still a common sight in New Hampshire.

The Way It Was . . . New Hampshire Government

New Hampshire has a long history of citizen involvement in its government. On January 5, 1776, six months before the Declaration of Independence was signed, New Hampshire set up a government completely independent from Britain. Today each of the state's 221 towns is almost entirely self-governing. Every four years, New Hampshire is the first state in the country to hold its United States presidential primary election. Before and during the primary, the eyes of the nation are focused on this New England state, a state that is small in size but rich in democratic spirit and pride.

A citizen speaks up during a town meeting.

Rocks and Forest

New Hampshire is known as the Granite State because of its large granite deposits. Some of this granite is quarried to produce stone for buildings. In the White Mountains, a natural granite formation that resembled the profile of a man's face was known as the Old Man of the Mountain before it collapsed in 2003. Forests cover more than 80 percent of New Hampshire. The state's trees include elms, maples, beeches, oaks, firs, and spruces. It's no wonder that New Hampshire is a leading producer of Christmas trees.

Above: The Old Man of the Mountain before its 2003 collapse. Inset: The mountain face today.

1808
Concord becomes
state capital

1852
Franklin Pierce elected
U.S. president

1934
World-record 231-mile-per-hour
wind gust at Mt. Washington

1996
Jeanne Shaheen elected
state's first woman governor

1838
First railroad in
New Hampshire
begins operation

1929
First U.S. ski school
opens in Franconia

1961
Alan Shepard, Jr. becomes
first American in space

2003
Old Man of the Mountain collapses;
work on memorial project begins

NEW JERSEY

The beautiful New Jersey shore

English settlers named New Jersey after the island of Jersey in the English Channel between England and France. The state — one of the 13 original colonies — is a peninsula bordered on the east and south by the Atlantic Ocean and on the west by the Delaware River. Although it is one of the smallest states in the nation, New Jersey shows stunning variety in its land and in the ways in which its people make a living.

Population and Industry

New Jersey has more people per square mile than any other state. The majority of those people live in northeastern New Jersey, across the Hudson River from New York City. This area is heavily industrialized. Almost every kind of product manufactured in the United States is made in New Jersey. Those products include cars, oil, telecommunications equipment, medicines, perfumes, chemicals, and much more.

Natural New Jersey

Despite its high population density, New Jersey has some wilderness areas. Northwestern New Jersey features rolling mountains, scenic valleys, rocky ridges, and lovely lakes. The Great Swamp, south of Morristown, is rich in wildlife. And the Pine Barrens in southern New Jersey is a large area of pine, oak, and cedar forests. In addition to the wilderness, New Jersey is known for its many fruit orchards and flower gardens. This explains why New Jersey is called the Garden State.

The Delaware Water Gap, where the Delaware River flows through a gorge

Princeton University is one of several institutions of higher learning located in New Jersey.

Timeline

1524
Giovanni da Verrazzano sails along New Jersey coast

1609
Henry Hudson lands in New Jersey

1676
New Jersey divided into East Jersey and West Jersey

1702
New Jersey becomes united British colony

1787
New Jersey becomes 3rd state

1790
Trenton becomes state capital

1838
Telegraph demonstrated near Morristown by Samuel F. B. Morse

1869
Campbell Soup Company established in Camden

NEW YORK

High Point 1,803 Ft. 550 M.

Delaware

Newton

Lake Hopatcong

Paterson

Morristown

Passaic

Phillipsburg

Newark

Jersey City

Irvington

Elizabeth

New York City

Perth Amboy

Edison

Raritan Bay

New Brunswick

Princeton

PENNSYLVANIA

Freehold

Trenton

Asbury Park

Burlington

Wrightstown

Philadelphia

Camden

Toms River

PINE BARRENS

Barnegat Bay

Wilmington

Glassboro

ATLANTIC OCEAN

DELAWARE

Hammonton

Bridgeton

Vineland

Great Bay

Millville

Atlantic City

0   10 Mi.
0   10 Km.

Delaware Bay

Wildwood

© Rand McNally
N-CUS27100-P1- -1- -1

Washington's boat dodges ice floes as it crosses the Delaware.

The Way It Was . . . Crossing the Delaware

Nearly 100 Revolutionary War battles were fought in New Jersey. One of the most famous began on Christmas night in 1776. On that stormy night, General George Washington and his band of 2,400 weary soldiers crossed the Delaware River from Pennsylvania to New Jersey. The next day, Washington's troops surprised and captured more than 900 enemy soldiers at Trenton and then marched on to successfully attack the British at Princeton. These victories in New Jersey gave Washington's troops much-needed supplies and revived their commitment to the Revolution.

The Wizard of Menlo Park

In 1876, a young inventor named Thomas Edison built his first research laboratory in Menlo Park, then a rural area south of Newark. There, Edison developed many of his 1,000-plus inventions, including the phonograph and the electric light bulb. Edison's most famous saying, "Genius is one percent inspiration and 99 percent per-spiration," reflected the way he worked. Today people can visit the Edison National Historic Site near Newark and view one of Edison's laboratories.

Thomas Edison speaks into one of his phonograph machines.

1927
Holland Tunnel linking New Jersey to New York City completed

1952
New Jersey Turnpike completed

1976
Casino gambling in Atlantic City begins

1998
New Jersey wins claim to most of Ellis Island

1921
Atlantic City hosts first Miss America pageant

1937
Hindenburg dirigible explodes over Lakehurst

1993
Christine Todd Whitman becomes New Jersey's first woman governor

NEW MEXICO

New Mexico gets its name from the bordering country of Mexico, to which New Mexico once belonged. The state's bright blue, seemingly endless sky and dramatic landscape have long inspired painters and photographers. The majestic, thickly forested Rocky Mountains reach their southernmost point in New Mexico. To the east and southeast lie the vast, relatively flat Great Plains, where cattle and sheep graze and crops such as cotton and wheat grow. West and southwest of the Rockies, the setting sun bathes the flat-topped mesas and the mountains in shades of pink, red, and purple.

Built by the Anasazi, Taos Pueblo is thought to be more than 600 years old.

Nature's Attractions

The Rio Grande flows through New Mexico from north to south. In the northern part of the state, the river has carved the spectacular Rio Grande Gorge. Carlsbad Caverns, one of the world's largest underground caves, features beautifully colored limestone formations that hang from the cave roof and rise from the cave floor. On summer evenings, thousands of bats create an amazing spectacle as they fly out of the cave in search of food.

Native Americans

When Spanish explorers arrived in New Mexico, they found Native Americans living in villages consisting of apartment-like buildings made of stone and adobe (sun-dried clay brick). The Spaniards dubbed the villages *pueblos*, which is Spanish for "towns." Today New Mexico is home to various groups of Pueblo Indians, most of whom still live in their ancestral villages. The largest pueblo is that of the Zuni, who are known for the beautiful jewelry they create from silver and turquoise.

White Sands National Monument near Alamogordo

Rug weaving is a longstanding tradition among the Navajo.

Timeline

1598
Juan de Onate establishes first Spanish colony in New Mexico

1610
Pedro de Peralta establishes capital at Santa Fe

1706
Albuquerque is founded

1821
New Mexico becomes a province of Mexico

1846
Start of Mexican War

1848
New Mexico becomes part of the U.S.

1850
Congress creates New Mexico Territory

1853
Gadsden Purchase enlarges New Mexico Territory

1878
Cattle ranchers start Lincoln County War

Centers of Culture and History

The ancestors of today's Pueblo Indians were the Anasazi. New Mexico's dry climate has helped preserve the Anasazi's imposing buildings, which can be seen today at such places as Aztec Ruins National Monument near Aztec. Modern Santa Fe is a major center for the arts. One museum there is devoted to the works of Georgia O'Keeffe, whose paintings of desert flowers, animal skulls, and landscapes in New Mexico appeal to a worldwide audience.

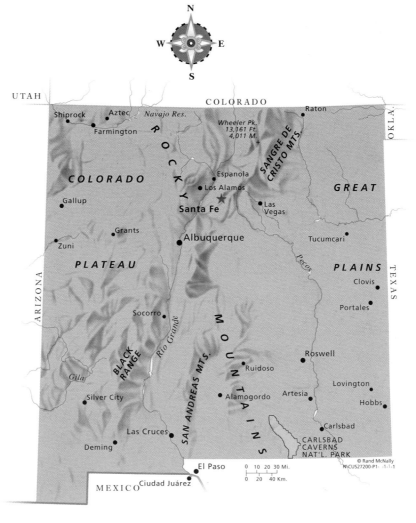

General Groves and Dr. Oppenheimer inspect the site of the first atomic bomb blast.

The Way It Was . . . Los Alamos

In 1942, with World War II raging, President Franklin D. Roosevelt approved a top-secret project to develop an ultra-powerful bomb. Perched atop a high mesa, the Los Alamos Ranch School for Boys provided the isolation needed for absolute secrecy. The government bought the school, made it into a laboratory, and brought in dozens of scientists. On July 16, 1945, the scientists tested the world's first atomic, or nuclear, bomb in the desert near Alamogordo. The explosion sent a mushroom cloud eight miles (13 kilometers) into the sky and tore a huge crater in the desert floor. Within weeks, United States planes dropped atomic bombs on the Japanese cities of Hiroshima and Nagasaki. World War II quickly came to an end.

Spectacular limestone formations in Carlsbad Caverns

State Facts

New Mexico Flag

Roadrunner

Yucca

Pinon Pine

Nickname
Land of Enchantment

Capital
Santa Fe

Area
121,356 square miles
(314,311 sq km)
Rank: 5th

Population
1,903,300
Rank: 36th

Statehood
January 6, 1912
47th state admitted

Principal Rivers
Rio Grande, Pecos River

Highest Point
Wheeler Peak,
13,161 feet (4,011 m)

Motto
Crescit eundo
(It grows as it goes)

Song
"Asi es Nuevo Mexico" and
"O, Fair New Mexico"

Famous People
John Denver,
Demi Moore,
Harrison Hagan Schmitt,
Al Unser

1912
New Mexico becomes 47th state

1930
Carlsbad Caverns National Park created

1948
Native Americans win right to vote in state elections

1997
Congressman Bill Richardson becomes U.S. ambassador to United Nations

1922
Oil discovered in San Juan and Eddy Counties

1945
World's first atomic bomb tested near Alamogordo

1988
Severe drought devastates New Mexico

1998
New Mexico celebrates 400th anniversary of Spanish colonization

NEW YORK

When people hear the name *New York*, they may think of New York City and the cities that surround it. But the state of New York is much more than cities — it is also mountains, seashores, waterfalls, and wilderness. Named after England's Duke of York, New York got its nickname, the "Empire State," from George Washington. He believed that the state could become the center of a new empire.

New York City

With more than eight million people, New York City — often called the Big Apple — is the largest city in the United States. In fact, this city has more people than do 41 of the 50 states. The city is home to immigrants from every part of the world. More than one-fifth of the people living in New York City in 1990 had been born in a country other than the United States, and one-fourth of the city's residents spoke a language other than English at home. New York City is a magnet for visitors as well as immigrants. Every year, 30 million tourists come to see such sites as the Empire State Building, Wall Street, and the Statue of Liberty. Tourists also enjoy museums, restaurants, and Broadway theaters. An important part of the city lies underground: 722 miles (1,155 kilometers) of subway lines carry millions of people around the city each week.

In 1886, France gave the Statue of Liberty to the United States as a gift symbolizing hope, freedom, and friendship.

Manhattan Bridge and Brooklyn skyline

Niagara Falls

Niagara Falls probably formed 12,000 years ago when glaciers melted and retreated. There are actually two parts to Niagara Falls: Horseshoe Falls is on the Canadian side, and American Falls is in New York. Every minute, 40 million gallons (152 million liters) of water pour over the two falls.

Niagara Falls has long been a sightseers' delight.

Timeline

1524 Giovanni da Verrazzano sails into New York Bay

1609 Henry Hudson explores Hudson River

1624 Dutch settlement established at present-day Albany

1626 Dutch governor Peter Minuit purchases Manhattan Island from Native Americans for $24

1664 English take control and name region New York

1785 New York City becomes capital of U.S.

1788 New York becomes 11th state

1789 George Washington inaugurated as first U.S. president in New York City

1825 Erie Canal completed

Map labels:

CANADA

St. Lawrence

Massena
Plattsburgh
Ogdensburg
Lake
Champlain

Watertown
Adirondack
Park
Mount
Marcy
5,344 Ft.
1,629 M.

VERMONT

ADIRONDACK
MOUNTAINS

Lake
George

LAKE ONTARIO

Oswego
Glens
Falls

Niagara
Falls
Lockport
Rochester
Rome
Black

N.Y. State Barge Canal
Syracuse
Utica

Niagara
Batavia
Auburn
MTS.
Mohawk

Buffalo
Genesee
Schenectady
Cooperstown
Troy
Albany

LAKE
ERIE
Gannett Hill
2,256 Ft.
688 M.
Dansville
Finger
Lakes
Ithaca
Oneonta
APPALACHIAN
TACONIC RANGE
MASS.

Dunkirk
Susquehanna

Jamestown
Olean
Elmira
Binghamton
CATSKILL
MTS.
Hudson

Allegheny Res.
PENNSYLVANIA
Delaware
Kingston

Poughkeepsie

Newburgh
CONN.
Middletown
West
Point

Yonkers
Long Island Sound
Montauk
NEW JERSEY
New York
LONG ISLAND
ATLANTIC OCEAN

N W E S

0 10 20 30 Mi.
0 10 20 30 40 Km.

Rand McNally
JS27300-P1- -1-1-1

Adirondack Park

Adirondack Park covers some six million acres (2.4 million hectares), or nearly a fifth of the state. The original forest preserve was mapped out in 1885. Seven years later, more land was added, and the decision was made to keep the park forever wild. The mountainous, heavily forested area is home to such animals as wild turkeys, beavers, moose, and black bears. It also features thousands of lakes, ponds, and streams, as well as the highest peak in the state, Mount Marcy.

The natural beauty of New York is on display in the rugged Adirondack Mountains.

The Way It Was...
The Big Ditch

In the early 1800s, the United States was rapidly expanding westward. Better transportation was needed between the East Coast and the western frontier lands. On July 4, 1817, work on the Erie Canal began. The canal would cross New York from the Hudson River to Lake Erie, linking the Atlantic Ocean to the Great Lakes. For eight years, thousands of men worked to finish what many called the Big Ditch. When it finally opened in 1825, the Erie Canal was a huge success. The costs of traveling and shipping goods across the state dropped, and cities sprang up along the canal and the Great Lakes.

The Erie Canal opens amidst great celebration and fanfare.

State Facts

New York Flag

Red-breasted Bluebird

Rose

Sugar Maple

Nickname
Empire State

Capital
Albany

Area
47,214 square miles
(122,284 sq km)
Rank: 30th

Population
19,227,100
Rank: 3rd

Statehood
July 26, 1788
11th state admitted

Principal Rivers
Hudson River,
St. Lawrence River

Highest Point
Mount Marcy,
5,344 feet (1,629 m)

Motto
Excelsior
(Ever upward)

Song
"I Love New York"

Famous People
Colin Powell,
Eleanor Roosevelt,
Franklin D. Roosevelt,
Theodore Roosevelt,
Jonas Salk

1831
First railroad in New York completed

1886
Statue of Liberty dedicated

1892
Ellis Island first used as immigration station

1929
Stock market crashes

2000
Yankees win third consecutive World Series

1883
Brooklyn Bridge opened

1901
President William McKinley assassinated in Buffalo

1989
Colin Powell becomes first African American to chair Joint Chiefs of Staff

2001
Terrorist attack destroys World Trade Center

NORTH CAROLINA

The colony of Carolina was named for King Charles I of England. (*Carolus* is the Latin version of "Charles.") In the early 1700s, the colony was split into North and South Carolina, and in 1789 North Carolina became a state. Textiles, tobacco, and furniture are some major products of modern-day North Carolina. Known for its diverse natural landscapes, North Carolina is also home to thriving cities, including Charlotte, one of the fastest-growing cities in the country.

Geography

North Carolina consists of three distinct geographic regions. The Atlantic Coastal Plain includes sand bars, known as the Outer Banks, that poke out into the ocean. Dangerous waters at Cape Hatteras have led to many shipwrecks, giving the area the nickname "Graveyard of the Atlantic." The hilly center of the state is known as the Piedmont. Most of North Carolina's people and industries are in the Piedmont. The western part of the state consists of Appalachian Mountain ranges, including the Great Smoky, Blue Ridge, Black, and Unaka Mountains.

True to their name, the Blue Ridge Mountains recede to the horizon in a series of blue ridges.

The Research Triangle

North Carolina's Research Triangle Park was established as a special place where people could work on and share their ideas. The park opened in 1959 and covers almost 7,000 acres (2,800 hectares). Unlike nature parks, this research park was designed to have many modern buildings in it. It is located in the area between three cities: Durham, Chapel Hill, and Raleigh. Each of these cities is home to a different famous university, and Raleigh is the capital of North Carolina. Well-known companies such as IBM, along with university and government people, conduct important research for business and industry in this convenient spot.

The Blue Ridge Parkway winds through the countryside of North Carolina.

Downtown Charlotte at night

Timeline

1524
Giovanni da Verrazzano explores North Carolina coast

1585
English settlers sent by Sir Walter Raleigh establish colony on Roanoke Island

1712
North and South Carolina become separate colonies

1729
North Carolina becomes a royal colony

1771
Soldiers led by royal governor defeat North Carolina rebels at Battle of Alamance

1774
Edenton Tea Party

1776
First battle of the Revolutionary War fought at Moore's Creek Bridge

1789
North Carolina becomes 12th state

VIRGINIA

TENNESSEE

Boone
Winston-Salem
Reidsville
Kerr Lake
Roanoke Rapids
Murfreesboro
Henderson
Elizabeth City
Kitty Hawk

Mt. Mitchell 6,684 Ft. 2,037 M.
BLUE RIDGE
PIEDMONT
Greensboro
High Pt.
Durham
Rocky Mount
Roanoke
Albemarle Sound
ROANOKE I.

GREAT SMOKY MTS. NAT'L. PARK
Morganton
Asheville
Lake Norman
Salisbury
Kannapolis
Chapel Hill
★ Raleigh

Sanford
Goldsboro

Murphy
Gastonia
Albemarle
High Rock Lake
Charlotte
Neuse
New Bern
Pamlico Sound
Cape Hatteras

GEORGIA
SOUTH CAROLINA
Fayetteville
Cape Fear
Lumberton

Cape Lookout

0 10 20 30 Mi.
0 20 40 Km.

Wilmington
ATLANTIC OCEAN

Cape Fear

State Facts

North Carolina Flag

Cardinal

Dogwood

Pine

Nickname
Tar Heel State

Capital
Raleigh

Area
48,711 square miles
(126,161 sq km)
Rank: 29th

Population
8,541,200
Rank: 11th

Statehood
November 21, 1789
12th state admitted

Principal Rivers
Roanoke River, Neuse River,
Cape Fear River

Highest Point
Mount Mitchell,
6,684 feet (2,037 m)

Motto
Esse quam videri
(To be rather than to seem)

Song
"The Old North State"

Famous People
Virginia Dare, Billy Graham,
Andy Griffith, Michael
Jordan, Dolley Madison

First in Flight

On December 17, 1903, the Wright brothers — Orville and Wilbur — made the world's first successful power-driven airplane flight near Kitty Hawk. Orville's first flight lasted 12 seconds, and Wilbur's lasted almost a minute. Five years and many experiments later, the Wrights had a contract with the federal government to make military airplanes. The Wright brothers' original planes are now on display in the National Air and Space Museum in Washington, D.C.

The first successful flight of the Wright brothers' plane

Settlers puzzle over the mysterious carving, the only clue left behind.

The Way It Was... The Lost Colony

One of the greatest unsolved mysteries in American history took place off the coast of North Carolina, on Roanoke Island. In 1585, the first English colony in North America was established on the island. The settlers, facing starvation, returned to England in 1586. The next year, a new group of more than 100 colonists arrived at Roanoke. The first English child in North America, Virginia Dare, was born there. The colony seemed secure this time. However, when a ship from England arrived with fresh supplies in 1590, the entire colony had disappeared. The new arrivals found only the word "CROATOAN" carved on a tree. The Croatoan Indians lived nearby, but no connection between them and the missing colonists was ever found. To this day, no one knows what became of the settlers who lived in the Lost Colony.

1898
Pepsi-Cola invented by Caleb Bradham in New Bern

1955
Hurricane Hazel

1960
Sit-in movement for civil rights begins in Greensboro

1996
Hurricanes Bertha and Fran

1997
Remains of pirate Blackbeard's ship discovered off coast

1903
Wright brothers' Kitty Hawk flights

1936
Intracoastal Waterway completed

1971
New state constitution goes into effect

1993
Eva Clayton and Mel Watt become first African Americans to represent the state in the U.S. House of Representatives since 1901

1999
Hurricane Floyd hits coast

NORTH DAKOTA

At the heart of North America sits the windswept state of North Dakota, named after the Sioux word for "friend" or "ally." Flat, rich farmland hugs the Red River along North Dakota's eastern border. Moving west across the Great Plains, the land rises and becomes drier. In the southwestern part of the state lie the Badlands. There wind and water have carved buttes (flat-topped hills) and other strangely beautiful formations out of rock and clay.

North Dakota Farms

In the late 1800s, huge wheat farms were developed in the Red River valley. Today, North Dakota produces more wheat than any other state except Kansas. Some of that is durum wheat, which is used in making spaghetti and other pasta. North Dakota farmers grow most of the durum wheat produced in the United States. Besides wheat, North Dakota's major crops include barley, flaxseed, rye, oats, sunflower seed, hay, and sugar beets.

Farmland in the fertile Red River Valley

The Badlands area of Theodore Roosevelt National Park

Parks

Established in 1932, the beautiful International Peace Garden straddles the border between North Dakota and Canada, honoring the friendship between the United States and Canada. In eastern North Dakota is Theodore Roosevelt National Park — the only national park named for a person. From 1884 to 1886, the man who would become the 26th president of the United States lived as a cattle rancher in what was then the Dakota Territory.

Timeline

1803
Southwestern North Dakota becomes part of U.S. through Louisiana Purchase

1818
Remainder of North Dakota becomes part of U.S.

1863
Homesteading begins in Dakota Territory

1738
Pierre Gaultier de Varennes, Sieur de La Verendrye, explores North Dakota

1812
First permanent European settlement at Pembina

1861
Congress creates Dakota Territory

1889
North Dakota becomes 39th state

1915
Arthur Charles Townley establishes Nonpartisan League

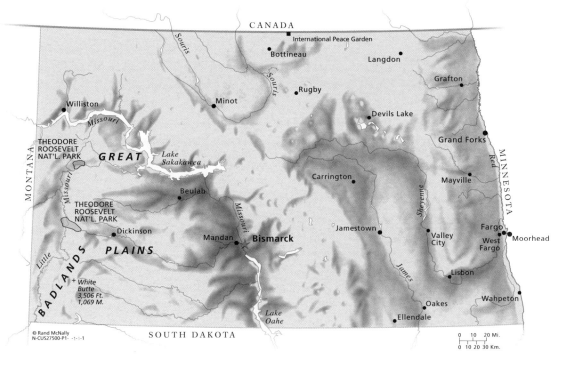

© Rand McNally
N-CUS27500-P1- -1-1-1

CANADA

SOUTH DAKOTA

State Facts

North Dakota Flag

Western Meadowlark

Wild Prairie Rose

American Elm

Nickname
Peace Garden State

Capital
Bismarck

Area
68,976 square miles
(178,647 sq km)
Rank: 17th

Population
634,400
Rank: 48th

Statehood
November 2, 1889
39th state admitted

Principal Rivers
Missouri River,
Red River

Highest Point
White Butte,
3,506 feet (1,069 m)

Motto
Liberty and union, now
and forever, one and
inseparable

Song
"North Dakota Hymn"

Famous People
Phil Jackson,
Louis L'Amour,
Peggy Lee,
Lawrence Welk

Statue of Sacagawea carrying her son Baptiste

The Way It Was . . . Lewis, Clark, and Sacagawea

In October 1804, an expedition led by Meriwether Lewis and William Clark reached the villages of a Native American tribe in what is now central North Dakota. The exhausted explorers built a camp, which they called Fort Mandan, and settled in for the winter. One day, a French-Canadian trader named Toussaint Charbonneau paid a visit. When the expedition set off again in April 1805, Charbonneau and his Shoshone wife, Sacagawea, went along as guides and interpreters. Carrying her infant son on her back, Sacagawea helped the explorers find food, saved supplies that accidentally washed overboard, and bargained with her fellow Shoshone for horses. Today a statue of Sacagawea stands outside North Dakota's capitol, in honor of the woman who contributed so much to the success of the Lewis and Clark expedition.

Wild Animals

North Dakota has so many flickertail ground squirrels that it is sometimes called the Flickertail State. Prairie dogs, which are related to ground squirrels, live in large underground colonies in the Badlands. Herds of buffalo roam the plains. Each summer, flocks of ducks and geese migrate to North Dakota to breed in the wetlands. In fact, more waterfowl hatch in North Dakota than in any other state.

1930
Major windstorm damages buildings and farms

1956
Garrison Dam generator begins to produce electricity

100 YEARS

1989
North Dakota centennial

2000
Rare red panda born in Fargo zoo

1951
Oil discovered at Williston Basin

1986
Garrison Diversion Project approved by Congress to increase water supply

1988
Devastating drought damages 3.5 million acres (1.4 million hectares)

1997
Red River flood causes billions in damages

OHIO

Ohio, known mainly for its manufacturing, is also home to a variety of other industries ranging from farming to tourism. The state got its name from the river that forms its southern and southeastern borders. The Iroquois Indians called the river *Ohio*, which means "big" or "great." Ohio is known as the Buckeye State for its once-plentiful buckeye, or horse chestnut, trees.

name comes from *nickname*

Ohio's Land and Water

Much of Ohio consists of plains, with some rugged hills and bluffs near the Kentucky and West Virginia borders. Ohioans have easy access to waterways for shipping goods: Their state is sandwiched between Lake Erie and the Ohio River and has more than 44,000 miles (70,800 kilometers) of rivers and streams. One of the state's most interesting landscape features was made by humans. A prehistoric group that historians call the Mound Builders created the Great Serpent Mound near Hillsboro. Viewed from overhead, the 1/4-mile-long (0.4-kilometer-long) earthen sculpture resembles a giant snake.

Cincinnati skyline

Birthplace of Astronauts

Ohio is the birthplace of more astronauts than any other state. More than 20 Ohioans have reached for the stars, including James A. Lovell, Neil A. Armstrong, and John H. Glenn. For one of these men, the lure of travelling in space once again was irresistible. After a successful political career as a senator from Ohio, Glenn returned to space aboard the shuttle *Discovery* in 1998, more than 30 years after he first orbited Earth.

The Rock and Roll Hall of Fame and Museum draws music fans from around the world.

Waterfall in Hocking Hills State Park

Timeline

1669
René-Robert Cavelier, Sieur de La Salle, explores region

1745
British build fort on Sandusky Bay

1763
Native Americans capture Fort Sandusky

1788
First permanent white settlement in Ohio, Marietta, is founded

1793
The *Centinel of the North-Western Territory*, first newspaper in the Northwest Territory, begins publication

1794
At Battle of Fallen Timber, U.S. troops defeat Native American forces

1803
Ohio becomes 17th state

1816
Columbus becomes state capital

Manufacturing Giant

Ohio is one of the most important manufacturing states in the country. One reason is the state's abundance of minerals such as coal, oil, natural gas, rock salt, and limestone. The state's ample water supplies and central location have also helped. Steel mills, automobile factories, oil refineries, and plants that make rubber, plastic, and chemicals have all played major roles in Ohio's economy. Two of the country's (and the world's) greatest industrial powerhouses began in Ohio in 1870: B. F. Goodrich Company, famous for its tires, and Standard Oil Company.

An illustration from an early edition of Uncle Tom's Cabin

The Way It Was...
Uncle Tom's Cabin

The Underground Railroad of the mid-1800s was not a real railroad with trains and tracks, but it did help people move from one place to another. A system of routes and hiding places, the Underground Railroad helped slaves escape from the South to the North or to Canada, where they could be free. The route across the Ohio River from Kentucky to Ohio was used frequently in the winter, because runaway slaves could walk across frozen sections of the river. One young woman was said to have crossed the river clutching a small child. She fell in the freezing water several times while struggling from one ice chunk to another. She arrived in Ohio drenched and shivering, just as slave catchers were closing in on her. This story was retold by Harriet Beecher Stowe in the 1852 novel *Uncle Tom's Cabin*. It is estimated that more than 100,000 slaves used the Underground Railroad to become free.

Cows graze in the lush pasture of an Ohio farm.

State Facts

Ohio Flag

Cardinal

Scarlet Carnation

Buckeye

Nickname
Buckeye State

Capital
Columbus

Area
40,948 square miles
(106,055 sq km)
Rank: 35th

Population
11,459,000
Rank: 7th

Statehood
March 1, 1803
17th state admitted

Principal Rivers
Ohio River, Scioto River

Highest Point
Campbell Hill,
1,549 feet (472 m)

Motto
With God, all things are possible

Song
"Beautiful Ohio"

Famous People
Neil Armstrong,
Halle Berry,
George Armstrong Custer,
Thomas Edison,
Arsenio Hall, Annie Oakley,
Steven Spielberg, R.L. Stine

1845
Miami and Erie Canal completed

1870
B. F. Goodrich opens a rubber-products plant in Akron

1969
Neil Armstrong walks on moon

1995
Rock and Roll Hall of Fame and Museum opens in Cleveland

1835
"Toledo War" dispute between Ohio and Michigan flares up

1868
Ohio native Ulysses Grant elected president of the U.S.

1955
Ohio Turnpike completed

1974
Tornado destroys much of Xenia

2003
Electrical problem in Ohio causes biggest blackout in North American history

OKLAHOMA

Prairie wildlife

Black Gold

Beneath Oklahoma's land lies a vast supply of oil, sometimes called "black gold" because of its color and the wealth it creates. Oil wells are found all over Oklahoma. Even the front lawn of the state capitol has oil wells. One of those wells drills at an angle to get oil from underneath the building. Oklahoma is also rich in another important mineral — natural gas.

Oklahoma is a land of plains and mountains, of prairie grasses and wheat fields, of armadillos and beef cattle. During the 1930s, some of the land literally blew away. A severe drought and high winds worked together to create the Dust Bowl, an area plagued by dust storms, which devastated the state's farmers. Oklahoma, however, is famous for much more than the Dust Bowl. The state's heritage is rich and varied, and Oklahoma still honors the different groups that contributed to its history, from Native Americans to pioneer farmers to cowboys.

Indian Territory

Between 1830 and 1842, the United States government forced most of the Native Americans living in the southeastern part of the country to move west to what the government called Indian Territory. One forced migration occurred during the winter of 1838-1839, when about 15,000 Cherokee were made to walk to Indian Territory. During this journey, known as the Trail of Tears, about 4,000 Cherokee died of starvation and other causes. When Indian Territory became a state in 1907, it was renamed Oklahoma, which means "red people" in the language of Choctaw Indians.

Working oil wells surround the capitol building.

Young cowboys compete in the International Finals Youth Rodeo.

Timeline

1541
Francisco Vásquez de Coronado explores Oklahoma

1682
René-Robert Cavelier, Sieur de La Salle, claims Oklahoma for France

1762
France cedes Oklahoma to Spain

1800
France regains Oklahoma

1803
Oklahoma becomes part of U.S. in Louisiana Purchase

1819
Most of Oklahoma becomes part of Arkansas Territory

1838-1839
Cherokee Trail of Tears

1889
First land run in Oklahoma

1890
Congress creates Territory of Oklahoma

COLORADO

Black Mesa
4,973 Ft.
1,516 M.

N. M.

TEXAS

KANSAS

MISSOURI

ARKANSAS

Guymon

Woodward

Alva

Cimarron

Enid

Ponca City

Kaw Lake

Bartlesville

Miami

Oologah Lake

Arkansas

Tulsa

Stillwater

Guthrie

Clinton

Washita

Oklahoma City

Shawnee

Norman

Canadian

Altus

Lawton

Duncan

Pauls Valley

Ada

McAlester

Okmulgee

Muskogee

Grand Lake O' The Cherokees

Eufaula Lake

Sardis Lake

OUACHITA MTS.

Lake Texoma

Durant

Red

Idabel

TEXAS

Red

© Rand McNally
N-CUS27700-P1- -1-1-1

0 10 20 30 Mi.
0 20 40 Km.

Rich Mountain, in southeastern Oklahoma's Ouachita National Forest

Green Country

Eastern Oklahoma is known for its rolling hills, river valleys, and forested mountain ridges. The Ozarks reach into the northeastern section, which is especially lush and has earned the nickname "Green Country." The Ouachita Mountains extend into southeastern Oklahoma. Lead, zinc, and timber are this rugged area's primary natural resources. Many tourists visits eastern Oklahoma to fish and camp, and also to boat on the large, beautiful reservoirs and lakes found throughout the area.

The Way It Was . . . The Land Runs

Settlers rush to the newly opened lands of central Oklahoma

By the late 1800s, white Americans living near Indian Territory wanted the area opened up to settlement. Bowing to their demands, the United States government declared that what is now central Oklahoma would become available at noon on April 22, 1889. As the day approached, settlers came to the edge of the region and waited. At the appointed hour, a gunshot signaled the beginning of a mad race as people dashed for land on which to build homes and to start farms. By the end of the day, about 50,000 settlers had staked claims, and brand new cities such as Enid, Guthrie, and Oklahoma City already held thousands of people. The land run of 1889 was the first of more than a dozen land openings in Indian Territory.

State Facts

Oklahoma Flag

Scissor-tailed Flycatcher

Mistletoe

Redbud

Nickname
Sooner State

Capital
Oklahoma City

Area
68,667 square miles
(177,847 sq km)
Rank: 19th

Population
3,523,600
Rank: 28th

Statehood
November 16, 1907
46th state admitted

Principal Rivers
Arkansas River, Canadian River, Red River

Highest Point
Black Mesa,
4,973 feet (1,516 m)

Motto
Labor omnia vincit
(Labor conquers all things)

Song
"Oklahoma"

Famous People
Garth Brooks,
Woody Guthrie,
Ron Howard,
Reba McEntire,
Brad Pitt,
Maria Tallchief

1897
First commercial oil well is drilled

1928
Vast oil field discovered near Oklahoma City

1995
Bombing of Alfred P. Murrah Federal Building

1999
Worst tornado in Oklahoma City history causes $1 billion damage

1907
Oklahoma becomes 46th state

1965
National Cowboy Hall of Fame opens

1997
Oklahoma celebrates 90th birthday

2003
Two major tornadoes strike Oklahoma City in two days

OREGON

Mount Hood towers over the city of Portland.

Wild Plants and Animals

Thick forests cover nearly half of Oregon. The state is best known for its evergreen trees. Some of Oregon's Douglas firs reach heights of 250 feet (76 meters). Oregon's wild flowering plants include azaleas and Oregon grape, which thrive in wet areas. In the dry east, plants like lupine, Indian paintbrush, and fireweed produce colorful blooms. Remains of prehistoric plants and animals can be seen at John Day Fossil Beds National Monument. The fossils include those of saber-toothed tigers and other creatures that roamed Oregon millions of years ago.

Scenic Oregon's Pacific coast features both white sand beaches and green mountains whose steep slopes rise abruptly from the shore. Breathtaking mountain scenery also is found in the Cascade Range, a chain of mountains named for its many cascading waterfalls. The Cascades divide Oregon into two main climate regions. Moist ocean winds bring moderate temperatures and much rain and snow to western Oregon, while eastern Oregon is drier and less mild. Fierce storms may have inspired early French trappers to give the name *Ouragan* — meaning "hurricane" — to

the river we now call the Columbia. Some historians believe that *Oregon* came from *Ouragon*.

Willamette Valley

Tucked between the Cascade and Coast Ranges is the fertile valley of the Willamette River. Most of Oregon's people live and work in the Willamette Valley. The explorers Lewis and Clark were enthusiastic about the valley. Their glowing reports excited other Americans, and thousands of settlers began to arrive in Oregon in the mid-1800s.

Crater Lake

McCall Park in downtown Portland

Timeline

1778
Captain James Cook sails along Oregon coast

1805
Lewis and Clark reach mouth of Columbia River

1811
Fort Astoria founded by John Jacob Astor

1829
Trading post opens at Willamette Falls

1834
First permanent American settlement established in Willamette Valley

1846
The *Oregon Spectator* first published

1848
Oregon becomes a U.S. territory

1850
Oregon Donation Land Law passed; gives land to settlers

The Map

Astoria
WASHINGTON
RANGES
Columbia
Portland
Hood River
The Dalles
Pendleton
La Grande
BLUE MOUNTAINS
McMinnville
Mt. Hood
11,239 Ft.
3,426 M.
Salem
Deschutes
John Day
COLUMBIA
Newport
Albany
Corvallis
Baker City
Snake
PACIFIC OCEAN
COAST
Prineville
PLATEAU
Springfield
Eugene
Bend
Ontario
Willamette
CASCADE RANGE
Burns
Malheur Lake
Lake Owyhee
IDAHO
Coos Bay
HARNEY BASIN
Roseburg
Harney Lake
Rogue
CRATER LAKE NATIONAL PARK
Owyhee
Upper Klamath Lake
Goose Lake
Brookings
Medford
Klamath Falls
Ashland
CALIFORNIA
NEVADA

0 10 20 30 Mi.
0 20 40 Km.

© Rand McNally
N-CUS27800-P1- -1-|-1

Making a Living

Oregon produces more lumber than any other state, as well as large quantities of paper and other forest products — including Christmas trees. Many Oregonians earn their living by farming. In addition to such products as wheat, potatoes, sheep, and cattle, Oregon farmers raise flower bulbs, grass seed, peppermint, and fruits like strawberries, pears, and wine grapes. Industries in Oregon range from the traditional, such as wood and food processing, to the high-tech, such as the production of computer components.

Stacks of logs await shipment in Astoria.

The Way It Was . . . Settlement and Conflict

Chief Joseph of the Nez Percé

In 1843, when Oregon was not yet a United States territory, covered wagons carrying the first large group of pioneers — about 900 people — arrived. By 1860, more than 250,000 people had traveled west on the 2,000-mile (3,200-kilometer) Oregon Trail. Settlers in the Oregon region soon came into conflict with the Native Americans who had lived there for generations. In 1847, a group of Cayuse killed missionaries Marcus and Narcissa Whitman and 12 others. The Cayuse were retaliating against a measles epidemic at the Whitman mission that had killed many Cayuse children. The murder of the Whitmans led to the Cayuse War of 1847-1848. Other wars followed. One of the last wars took place in 1877, when a group of Nez Percé, led by Chief Joseph, resisted a government order to leave their northeastern Oregon homes. The Nez Percé fought the army and tried to escape to Canada but eventually were forced to surrender.

State Facts

Oregon Flag

Western Meadowlark

Oregon Grape

Douglas Fir

Nickname
Beaver State

Capital
Salem

Area
95,997 square miles
(248,631 sq km)
Rank: 10th

Population
3,594,600
Rank: 27th

Statehood
February 14, 1859
33rd state admitted

Principal Rivers
Columbia River,
Willamette River

Highest Point
Mount Hood,
11,239 feet (3,426 m)

Motto
The Union

Song
"Oregon, My Oregon"

Famous People
Beverly Cleary,
Chief Joseph,
Matt Groening,
Linus Pauling

Timeline

1851 First public school in Oregon established

1859 Oregon becomes 33rd state

1937 Bonneville Dam completed on Columbia River

1985 State lottery established

1998 Oregon institutes voting by mail, eliminating polling places

1855 Salem becomes state capital

1933 Tillamook Burn forest fire

1967 Astoria Bridge links Oregon and Washington

1993 150th anniversary of Oregon Trail

PENNSYLVANIA

In 1681, King Charles II of England gave the land that would become Pennsylvania to William Penn. Penn named the area *Sylvania*, from the Latin word for "woods," and the name eventually became *Pennsylvania*, or "Penn's Woods." Even today, 60 percent of the state is covered by forests.

Philadelphia and Pittsburgh

Philadelphia, Pennsylvania's largest city, is the fifth largest city in the country and the site of many key events in United States history. Modern-day visitors can tour Independence Hall, where both the Declaration of Independence and the United States Constitution were signed. The Liberty Bell is nearby, as is Carpenters' Hall, site of the First Continental Congress. Pittsburgh, the state's second largest city, has historically been home to heavy industry, especially steel production. Today both cities have beautiful downtown areas and support a variety of industries and cultural institutions.

Fireworks explode over Independence Hall, where the Second Continental Congress met during the Revolutionary War.

Gettysburg

Gettysburg National Military Park is the site of one of the bloodiest battles of the Civil War. About 7,000 soldiers lost their lives in the battle, which took place in July of 1863. The Battle of Gettysburg was a big win for the Union forces and a turning point in the war. Four months after the battle, President Abraham Lincoln gave his now-famous Gettysburg Address to dedicate part of the battlefield as a cemetery. Today, visitors wander the grounds, which feature thousands of grave markers memorializing the lives lost.

Philadelphia

President Lincoln delivers the Gettysburg Address on November 19, 1863.

Timeline

1615
Cornelius Hendricksen sails up Delaware River to what is now Philadelphia

1643
First permanent European settlement established, on Tinicum Island

1681
King Charles II grants Pennsylvania to William Penn

1758
Fort Pitt established

1776
Declaration of Independence signed

1787
U.S Constitution signed; Pennsylvania becomes 2nd state

1812
Harrisburg becomes state capital

1859
Country's first oil we drilled near Titusville

LAKE ERIE

Erie

Bradford
Allegheny
Reservoir

NEW YORK

Sayre

Meadville

Pymatuning
Res.

Oil City

Scranton

Williamsport

Wilkes-Barre

New Castle

Du Bois

OHIO

State College

Hazleton

NEW JERSEY

Butler

Indiana

Lewistown

Pottsville

Bethlehem

Ohio

Altoona

Allentown

Pittsburgh

McKeesport

Latrobe

Johnstown

Reading

Lebanon

Pottstown

Washington

Harrisburg

Lancaster

Philadelphia

Uniontown

Mt. Davis
3,213 Ft.
979 M.

Chambersburg

York

Coatesville

Chester

Delaware

W. VIRGINIA

Gettysburg

Hanover

Wilmington

© Rand McNally
N-CUS27900-P1- -1-1-1

Hagerstown

MARYLAND

DEL.

0 10 20 Mi.
0 10 20 30 Km.

State Facts

Pennsylvania Flag

Ruffed Grouse

Mountain Laurel

Hemlock

Nickname
Keystone State

Capital
Harrisburg

Area
44,817 square miles
(116,076 sq km)
Rank: 32nd

Population
12,406,300
Rank: 6th

Statehood
December 12, 1787
2nd state admitted

Principal Rivers
Allegheny River,
Delaware River,
Ohio River,
Susquehanna River

Highest Point
Mount Davis,
3,213 feet (979 m)

Song
"Pennsylvania"

Motto
Virtue, liberty,
and independence

Famous People
Louisa May Alcott,
Mary Cassatt, Bill Cosby,
Robert Peary,
Fred Rogers

The Way It Was . . . Writing the Constitution

Throughout the hot summer of 1787, George Washington, Benjamin Franklin, and other delegates to the Constitutional Convention gathered at the State House (now Independence Hall) in Philadelphia to debate and create a constitution for the new nation. On September 15, the delegates approved the final draft and sent it to be embossed, or formally penned. Jacob Sallus, a Revolutionary War veteran and an assistant clerk for the Pennsylvania General Assembly, was given the job. Using a goose feather dipped in ink, he transcribed the document onto sheets of parchment. The delegates signed this document on September 17, thus creating the foundation of American government and law.

Washington speaks to the convention delegates.

Amish Country

Among the people who emigrated to Pennsylvania in the late 1600s and the 1700s were members of several religious groups from Germany and Switzerland. These groups included the Mennonites, Moravians, Dunkers, and Amish. They were called the Plain People because of their plain clothes and simple lives. Today the Plain People, most of them Amish, live much as their ancestors did on farms near Lancaster.

An Amish farmer

1879
Frank W. Woolworth opens first dime store

1905
Hershey chocolate plant established

1979
Three Mile Island nuclear plant accident

2004
Civil rights activist Dr. Dorothy Height receives Congressional Gold Medal

1863
Battle of Gettysburg; Lincoln gives Gettysburg Address

1889
Johnstown flood disaster

1956
Pennsylvania Turnpike completed

1985
Deadly tornado outbreak

RHODE ISLAND

Rhode Island is the smallest state in the country. Sometimes called Little Rhody, it is only 40 miles (64 kilometers) wide at its widest point. Despite its small size, Rhode Island has 384 miles (614 kilometers) of shoreline and 36 offshore islands. Although no one is sure, some think that the name *Rhode Island* comes from *Roodt Eylandt*, which means "red island" in Dutch. A Dutch sailor gave this name to an island in Narragansett Bay because of the red clay he saw on the island's shore.

The Coast

Each summer Rhode Island's beautiful coast attracts hundreds of thousands of sightseers as well as boaters, fishermen, and other water-sports enthusiasts. Despite its appeal, the coast can be dangerous: Twenty lighthouses have been built along Rhode Island's shores to warn sailors of treacherous rocks in the water. The coastal town of Newport is home to mansions built as summer homes in the 1800s and early 1900s by wealthy families. Some of these homes have been turned into museums. The most famous of the mansions is the Breakers, built by Cornelius Vanderbilt in 1895.

The Breakers is a National Historic Landmark.

The city of Providence at dusk

Spinning Jenny

Rhode Island was one of the first states to develop a strong manufacturing presence. This was due in part to the introduction in the United States of the spinning jenny, a device that spun cotton into thread. Samuel Slater, using only his memory of the device from his time in England, built the country's first water-powered spinning jennies in Pawtucket in 1790. With its abundance of water power, Rhode Island quickly became a leader in the textile industry.

Timeline

1524 Giovanni da Verrazzano explores Narragansett Bay

1636 Roger Willams establishes first permanent settlement at Providence

1638 Anne Hutchinson and others settle Portsmouth

1675 Great Swamp Fight between colonists and Native Americans

1699 Quakers set up first meetinghouse in Newport

1763 Touro Synagogue built in Newport

1764 Brown University founded as Rhode Island College

1776 Rhode Island is first colony to for declare independence from Engl

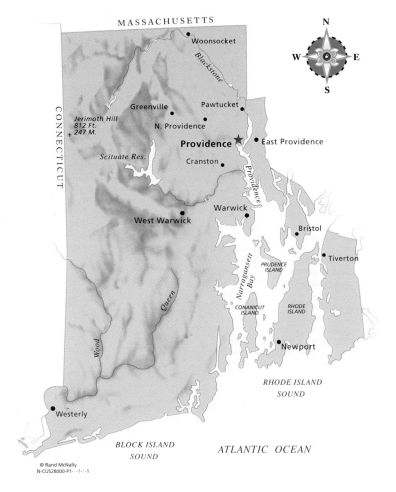

MASSACHUSETTS

Woonsocket

CONNECTICUT

Greenville

Jerimoth Hill
812 Ft.
247 M.

N. Providence

Pawtucket

Providence

East Providence

Scituate Res.

Cranston

Warwick

West Warwick

Bristol

Tiverton

Narragansett Bay

PRUDENCE ISLAND

CONANICUT ISLAND

RHODE ISLAND

Wood

Queen

Newport

RHODE ISLAND SOUND

Westerly

BLOCK ISLAND SOUND

ATLANTIC OCEAN

© Rand McNally
N-CUS28000-P1- -1-|-1

BLOCK ISLAND

| 0 | 2 | 4 | 6 | 8 | 10 Mi. |
| 0 | | 5 | | 10 Km. | |

The Way It Was . . . Roger Williams

In 1636, Puritan minister Roger Williams and a few followers fled Massachusetts, where Williams had criticized leaders for their lack of religious tolerance. Williams's group came to Rhode Island, developing a friendly relationship with the Narragansett tribe and founding Providence. By 1643, there were three other settlements in Rhode Island. Some colonists in neighboring Massachusetts wanted to take over the successful Rhode Island settlements. Knowing this, Williams suggested that the four settlements unite for protection, which they did in 1647. In 1663, England's King Charles II granted the combined settlement a royal charter, which served as the law in Rhode Island for 180 years.

Roger Williams braves the wind as he heads into exile.

Economy

One-fifth of Rhode Island's economy is tied to manufacturing. Textiles, electronics, and jewelry are some of the goods produced in the state. Fishing, while not as important an industry as it is in other coastal states, still produces tens of millions of dollars in income. Rhode Island's farmers produce fruits, vegetables, plants, milk, and poultry. But service industries — including services for tourists — form the backbone of the state's economy.

More than 400 miles (640 km) of coastline invite sailors and other maritime adventurers to explore Rhode Island.

State Facts

Rhode Island Flag

Rhode Island Red

Violet

Red Maple

Nickname
Ocean State

Capital
Providence

Area
1,045 square miles
(2,707 sq km)
Rank: 50th

Population
1,080,600
Rank: 43rd

Statehood
May 29, 1790
13th state admitted

Principal Rivers
Blackstone River,
Providence River

Highest Point
Jerimoth Hill,
812 feet (247 m)

Motto
Hope

Song
"Rhode Island"

Famous People
William Anders,
Nicholas Brown,
George M. Cohan,
Leonard Woodcock

1835
First railroad service in
Rhode Island begins

1883
Newport Naval Station
opened by U.S. Navy

1973
Quonset Point Naval
Air Station closes

2002
350th anniversary of first
U.S. law against slavery

1790
Rhode Island is last to ratify
U.S. Constitution; becomes
13th state

BALLOTS

1842
Dorr Rebellion for
voting rights
begins

1969
Newport Bridge over
Narragansett Bay
opens

1990
Rhode Island celebrates
200th anniversary

SOUTH CAROLINA

South Carolina was once part of Carolina, a colony named after King Charles I of England. In 1712 North and South Carolina became separate colonies, and South Carolina became a state in 1788. South Carolina's warm, wet climate supports a variety of plant life, from peach trees grown by farmers to wild cypresses, Spanish moss, and palmettos, a type of palm tree. In fact, South Carolina is nicknamed the Palmetto State. Palmettos are not only attractive but useful. During the Revolutionary War, for example, soldiers in South Carolina used them to make forts. British cannonballs practically bounced off the strong fort walls.

Geography

The beautiful Blue Ridge Mountains cover the northwestern corner of South Carolina. East of the mountains lies the hilly Piedmont. South Carolinians call the Blue Ridge Mountains and the Piedmont the Up Country. The Atlantic Coastal Plain, which covers southeastern South Carolina, is home to farms where tobacco, soybeans, and other crops are grown. South Carolinians call the area nearest the coast the Low Country. The state's long coastline is called the Grand Strand of Sand. Sandy beaches such as Myrtle Beach help make South Carolina's coastline a popular vacation area.

Colorful Rainbow Row in Charleston

Charleston

Charleston's location on a harbor of the Atlantic Ocean has long made it a busy port. Founded in 1670 as Charles Towne, after King Charles II, the city was renamed Charleston in 1783. Lovely homes dating from the 1700s and 1800s still line many of the city's streets. Charleston is also home to the Old Slave Mart, where African slaves were once sold. Today the building is a museum with artifacts depicting the horrors of the slave trade, including the conditions that slaves endured in cramped ships on the way to America.

Hilton Head Island was named after Captain William Hilton, a British sailor in the 1600s.

Timeline

1521
Francisco Gordillo explores the coast of South Carolina

1670
Albemarle Point is site of first permanent European settlement in South Carolina

1719
South Carolina becomes a royal colony

1788
South Carolina becomes eighth state

1800
Santee Canal completed

1824
The Citadel military college is founded

1828
South Carolina native Andrew Jackson elected president of U.S.

1861
Confederates attack Fort Sumter; Civil War begins

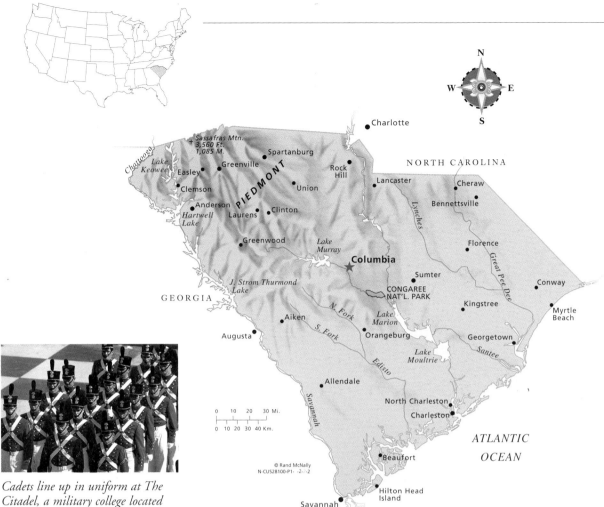

© Rand McNally
N-CUS28100-P1- -2- -2

Cadets line up in uniform at The Citadel, a military college located in Charleston.

State Facts

South Carolina Flag

Carolina Wren

Carolina Jessamine

Palmetto

Nickname
Palmetto State

Capital
Columbia

Area
30,109 square miles
(77,982 sq km)
Rank: 40th

Population
4,198,100
Rank: 25th

Statehood
May 23, 1788
8th state admitted

Principal Rivers
Savannah River,
Great Pee Dee River

Highest Point
Sassafras Mountain,
3,560 feet (1,085 m)

Mottos
Animis opibusque parati
(Prepared in mind
and resources);
Dum spiro spero
(While I breathe, I hope)

Song
"South Carolina on
My Mind"

Famous People
Joe Frazier, Andrew
Jackson, Jesse Jackson,
Strom Thurmond

The Way It Was... Denmark Vesey

Denmark Vesey was a slave owned by Joseph Vesey, the captain of a slave-trading ship. Denmark worked on the ship and saw firsthand the awful conditions that the slaves endured on their trip from Africa to America. When Joseph Vesey retired in 1783, he set up a carpentry business in Charleston and taught Denmark carpentry skills. In 1799 Denmark Vesey won $1,500 in a lottery. With his winnings, he purchased his freedom and a small home for himself, but he longed to help other African Americans who were less fortunate. In 1822 Vesey organized about 9,000 slaves and free African Americans to carry out a revolt to free slaves in South Carolina. However, plans for the revolt were leaked to authorities, and Vesey and some members of his group were caught and put on trial. At 54 years of age, Vesey was executed for the crime of trying to gain for others the freedom that he had enjoyed.

Slaves being sold at auction in Charleston

Textiles

Textile production is South Carolina's leading industry. Many kinds of products found in people's homes are textiles. Carpeting, curtain fabric, bedsheets, and tablecloths are examples of products made by South Carolina's textile companies. About one-quarter of all the people who have jobs in South Carolina help make textiles.

Uploading fabric in a textile mill

1886
Earthquake kills 92 in Charleston

1893
Hurricane causes over 1,000 deaths

1921
Boll weevils destroy much of the state's cotton crop

1941
Santee Dam provides state's first hydroelectric power

1953
Savannah River Plant begins producing nuclear materials

1989
Hurricane Hugo causes over $5 billion in damage

2002
Strom Thurmond, longest-serving U.S. senator, retires

2004
Record number of tornadoes spawned by tropical storms

SOUTH DAKOTA

South Dakota is a state divided in two by the mighty Missouri River. East of the river, glaciers of the Ice Age created gently rolling land covered with rich soil and dotted by lakes. Most of South Dakota's cities, towns, and crop farms are found in this region. West of the Missouri River, the land becomes higher and rougher and is mostly covered by sprawling ranches. Far to the west rise the beautiful Black Hills, named for the evergreen trees that make the slopes appear black from a distance. Southeast of the Black Hills are the Badlands, a nearly barren but stunning area of multicolored rock carved into odd shapes by erosion.

Two Dakotas

South Dakota shares much with neighboring North Dakota. Both states were once part of the Dakota Territory, which got its name from the Sioux word for "friend" or "ally." Both Dakotas became states the same day; South Dakota is considered the 40th state only because it comes after North Dakota in the alphabet.

The Badlands offer an awe-inspiring landscape of colorful buttes and sweeping grasslands.

South Dakota Attractions

Mount Rushmore National Memorial, in the Black Hills, is South Dakota's most famous attraction. It features the massive carved faces of four U.S. presidents: George Washington, Thomas Jefferson, Theodore Roosevelt, and Abraham Lincoln. However, there are many other things to see in South Dakota. West of Mount Rushmore is Crazy Horse Memorial. Its focal point is a huge carving-in-progress of the Sioux leader Crazy Horse, who was killed in 1877. Once completed, the sculpture will be so large that all four Mount Rushmore heads could easily fit into Crazy Horse's head. Deadwood, near Lead, is another tourist attraction. After gold was discovered in the Black Hills in 1874, prospectors and settlers poured in. Boomtowns like Deadwood soon sprang up. Today's Deadwood has replicas of old-time saloons as well as the cemetery in which Wild Bill Hickok and Calamity Jane are both buried.

Mount Rushmore

Timeline

1743
Francois and Louis Joseph de la Verendrye are first white explorers to reach South Dakota

1817
Fort Pierre becomes first permanent settlement in South Dakota

1874
Gold discovered in Black Hills

1682
René-Robert Cavelier, Sieur de La Salle, claims land for France

1803
U.S. acquires South Dakota through Louisiana Purchase

1861
Congress establishes Dakota Territory

1889
South Dakota becomes 40th state

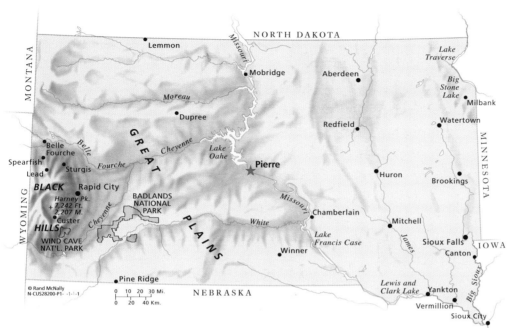

© Rand McNally
N-CUS28200-P1- -1-1-1

0 10 20 30 Mi.
0   20   40 Km.

State Facts

South Dakota Flag

Chinese Ring-necked Pheasant

Pasque Flower

Black Hills Spruce

Nickname
Mount Rushmore State

Capital
Pierre

Area
75,885 square miles
(196,541 sq km)
Rank: 16th

Population
770,900
Rank: 46th

Statehood
November 2, 1889
40th state admitted

Principal Rivers
James River,
Missouri River

Highest Point
Harney Peak,
7,242 feet (2,207 m)

Motto
Under God the
people rule

Song
"Hail, South Dakota"

Famous People
L. Frank Baum,
Tom Brokaw,
Hubert H. Humphrey,
Sitting Bull

The South Dakota state capitol was built between 1905 and 1910.

Sitting Bull, whose Sioux name was Tatanka Iyotake

The Way It Was . . . Wounded Knee

In 1890, United States army leaders ordered the arrest of Sioux leader Sitting Bull, who was then living on Standing Rock Reservation in the northern part of South Dakota. As police tried to arrest him, Sitting Bull was killed. Alarmed, some of his followers fled south and joined another group of Sioux. Cold weather drove them to the Pine Ridge Reservation in the very southern part of the state. Soldiers caught up with them there and on December 29, near Wounded Knee Creek, a massacre began. The soldiers killed as many as 300 Sioux men, women, and children. Twenty-five soldiers also were killed, most by army crossfire. This tragedy marked the end of the long war between the Sioux and the United States army.

Tapping Natural Resources

Since it opened in 1876, the Homestake Mine in Lead has produced more gold than any other mine in the world. The mine still has millions of tons of the precious mineral. Although less glamorous than gold, the soil of South Dakota is its most important resource. The eastern soil is well-suited for growing corn, wheat, and soybeans. The western soil makes good grazing land for beef cattle and sheep.

1889
Pierre becomes
state capital

1890
Massacre at
Wounded
Knee Creek

1927
Gutzon Borglum begins
work on Mount Rushmore
National Memorial

1944
Missouri River Basin Project
approved by Congress

1973
Wounded Knee village
occupied by Native
American group for 71 days

1980
State ordered to pay Sioux
for land seized in 1877

1993
Severe flooding causes crop damage of more than $725 million

2003
South Dakota tries to recruit dairy
farmers from United Kingdom to
increase state production

TENNESSEE

Replica of Greece's Parthenon in Nashville

A bluish haze hangs over Clingmans Dome, the highest peak in Tennessee.

Music City, U.S.A.

Located in the center of the state, Tennessee's capital, Nashville, is nicknamed Music City, U.S.A. Nashville is home to dozens of recording studios, as well as the Grand Ole Opry House, a theater that is famous for its country music shows. In fact, Nashville is widely regarded as the country music capital of the world.

Tennessee's beautiful and varied landscape includes rugged mountains, broad valleys, lush forests, and sparkling waters. Tennessee culture — especially Tennessee music — is just as diverse. The state's musical gifts to the world range from country tunes performed at the Grand Ole Opry to the Memphis rock-and-roll songs of Elvis Presley. Long before Tennessee produced such music, it was home to the Cherokee. The name *Tennessee* comes from the name of one Cherokee village, Tanasie. Tennessee is also called the Volunteer State, because so many of its people have volunteered to fight in the country's wars.

Three Stars, Three Parts

The three stars on Tennessee's flag represent the state's three distinct land regions. One star represents the Blue Ridge and Great Smoky Mountains in the eastern part of the state. Great Smoky Mountains National Park attracts more visitors than any other national park. Another star on Tennessee's flag represents central Tennessee, covered by gently rolling land. There, sheep, horses, and cattle graze on bluegrass. The last star on Tennessee's flag represents the western part of the state, which lies between the Tennessee and Mississippi Rivers. The lowlands of this area have many cotton and soybean fields.

A band entertains the crowd at the Grand Ole Opry.

Timeline

1540
Hernando de Soto leads first white expedition

1775
Daniel Boone blazes trail through Cumberland Gap

1779
Jonesborough is founded

1780
Cumberland Compact signed by Nashville settlers

1784
East Tennessee forms its own country, the Republic of Franklin

1796
Tennessee becomes the 16th state

1838
Cherokee Indians forced out of Tennessee

1843
Nashville becomes state capital

1861
Tennessee is last state to secede from Union

1862
Battle of Shiloh

Tennessee Flag

Mockingbird

Iris

Tulip Poplar

Nickname
Volunteer State

Capital
Nashville

Area
41,217 square miles
(106,752 sq km)
Rank: 34th

Population
5,901,000
Rank: 16th

Statehood
June 1, 1796
16th state admitted

Principal Rivers
Mississippi River,
Tennessee River

Highest Point
Clingmans Dome,
6,643 feet (2,025 m)

Motto
Agriculture and commerce

Song
"The Tennessee Waltz" and
four others

Famous People
Roy Acuff,
James Agee,
Dorothy Brown,
Davy Crockett,
Albert Gore,
Cordell Hull

Norris Dam, built in 1936, was one of the first dams constructed by the Tennessee Valley Authority.

Davy Crockett

The Way It Was... Davy Crockett

Explorer, soldier, hunter, congressman — Davy Crockett played all these roles during his life. Using the saying "Be sure you're right, then go ahead" as his guide, Crockett chased after his many goals. Crockett was born in the Great Smoky Mountains in 1786. Today visitors can tour his birthplace in Limestone. Although Tennessee is known as the Volunteer State, Crockett called the area "the Shakes" because of the strong earthquakes that rocked the state in 1811-1812. Although he spent much of his time exploring and living in the outdoors, Crockett eventually gained a more civilized image. He became a member of the United States Congress, serving three terms.

Memphis

Memphis, Tennessee's largest city, looks out over the Mississippi River. The city was named after the ancient Egyptian city of Memphis, which was also located on a mighty river, the Nile. Shipping is very important in Memphis. Goods are transported on the Mississippi, by six major railroads, over nine major highways, and through one of the world's busiest cargo airports. Memphis isn't all business, though. Known as one of the birthplaces of the blues, Memphis was also home to rock-and-roll legend Elvis Presley.

Memphis

1866
Tennessee first state
to return to Union

1933
Congress creates Tennessee
Valley Authority

1968
Martin Luther King, Jr.
assassinated in Memphis

1991
National Civil Rights
Museum opens

1864
Battle of
Nashville

1878
Yellow fever epidemic
wipes out 25% of
Memphis' population

1928
Grand Ole
Opry begins

1942
Construction begins
on atomic energy
center at Oak Ridge

1982
World's Fair
held in
Knoxville

2000
Albert Gore loses to George W. Bush
in hotly contested presidential election

TEXAS

Texas is big. It covers one-twelfth of the land in the 48 contiguous states. Only Alaska has more land than Texas and only California more people. Texas has two of the country's ten largest cities: Houston and Dallas. A place the size of Texas is bound to look very different from one area to another. For example, the lush forests along the Louisiana border contrast sharply with the high, dry *Llano Estacado* (Staked Plain) of the Panhandle. Texas takes its name from the word *tejas*, a Spanish version of a Native American word meaning "friends" or "allies."

The "world's largest cowboy boots" can be found at the North Star shopping mall in San Antonio.

Cattle and Oil

Raising cattle became big business in Texas in the 1860s, when cowboys began driving huge herds of longhorns along trails such as the Chisholm. Texas still leads all states in beef cattle production. In 1901, oil began to gush from a well on Spindletop, a hill near Beaumont. Thanks to Spindletop and other major oil finds, Texas has been enriched by its natural resources. Today Texas still produces more oil and more natural gas than any other state.

Tex-Mex Culture

For hundreds of years, Texas has had close ties with Mexico, its neighbor across the Rio Grande. Both were once part of Spain's vast empire in the Americas. When Mexico gained its independence in 1821, Texas came under Mexican rule. That didn't last long, but the blending of people and ways of life has never stopped. About 20 percent of all Texans are Mexican Americans, and "Tex-Mex" influence is evident everywhere. From music to food — such as spicy chili and breakfast tacos — Tex-Mex culture is a significant part of Texas's identity.

The beautiful Hill Country of south-central Texas

Mexican folk dancers at a festival in Texas

Timeline

1519
Alonso Alvarez de Pineda lands on Texas coast

1685
René-Robert Cavelier, Sieur de La Salle, founds Fort St. Louis

1718
Alamo mission established at San Antonio

1835
Beginning of Texas Revolution

1836
Texas becomes Republic of Texas

1845
Texas becomes 28th state

1861
Texas joins the Confederacy

1870
Texas readmitted to the Union

© Rand McNally
N-CUS28400-P1- -1- -1

Texas Flag

Mockingbird

Bluebonnet

Pecan

Nickname
Lone Star State

Capital
Austin

Area
261,797 square miles
(678,052 sq km)
Rank: 2nd

Population
22,490,000
Rank: 2nd

Statehood
December 29, 1845
28th state admitted

Principal Rivers
Pecos River,
Red River,
Rio Grande

Highest Point
Guadalupe Peak,
8,749 feet (2,667 m)

Motto
Friendship

Song
"Texas, Our Texas"

Famous People
Carol Burnett,
George W. Bush,
Lyndon B. Johnson,
Scott Joplin,
Willie Nelson

Houston's skyline

The Alamo

The Way It Was . . . The Alamo

In 1836, the most famous battle for Texas independence from Mexico took place in San Antonio. There about 200 Texan rebels were holed up in an old mission called the Alamo. For days, Mexican soldiers led by General Antonio Lopez de Santa Anna fired on the mission. Then, on March 6, Mexicans charged and fought the Texans hand-to-hand. All of the Alamo's defenders, including Colonel William B. Travis and frontier legends Jim Bowie and Davy Crockett, were killed in the battle or executed soon after. The defeat at the Alamo only hardened the Texans' determination. On April 21, Texan soldiers led by General Sam Houston surprised Santa Anna near present-day Houston. With shouts of "Remember the Alamo!" the Texans defeated Santa Anna's forces and won independence for Texas.

Texas Cities

Each of Texas's three largest cities is unique and important. In Houston, the Lyndon B. Johnson Space Center controls all piloted space missions launched by NASA — the National Aeronautics and Space Administration. San Antonio, an important manufacturing and trade center, is also a popular tourist destination. The glittering skyscrapers of Dallas are home to banking, insurance, oil, and other businesses. And Dallas-Fort Worth International Airport is one of the busiest airports in the world.

1936
Texas Centennial
Exposition

1963
President John F. Kennedy assassinated in
Dallas; Lyndon B. Johnson becomes president

1989
Former Texas oilman George H.W.
Bush becomes president

1901
Oil discovered at
Beaumont

1962
Lyndon B. Johnson Space Center
(originally Manned Spacecraft
Center) built in Houston

1965
Astrodome opens
in Houston

2004
George W. Bush elected to
second presidential term

UTAH

Thousands of years ago, what is now Utah was partly covered by a vast freshwater sea. Utah's best-known natural feature, the Great Salt Lake, is in a sense a leftover of that ancient sea. West and southwest of the lake lie Utah's deserts, which stand in sharp contrast to the snowcapped Rocky Mountains in the northeast. Utah's southeast corner touches the corners of Arizona, New Mexico, and Colorado at Four Corners — the only place in the United States where four states meet. Utah takes its name from the Ute, a Native American tribe.

Salt Lake City and the Wasatch Mountains

Natural Wonders

Streams bring fresh water into the Great Salt Lake, but a lack of streams flowing out means the water has nowhere to drain. Instead it evaporates, leaving behind salt and other minerals that have been dissolved in the water. In Bryce Canyon National Park, unusual rock formations, in colors ranging from red to cream, rise from the floors of deep valleys. Arches National Park is home to thousands of sandstone formations that resemble giant arches, windows, and towers.

Reminders of the Past

Utah's early Native American groups included the Anasazi, who often built homes on high canyon walls. Their cliff dwellings can be seen in such places as Capitol Reef National Park. Golden Spike National Historic Site honors the completion of the country's first coast-to-coast railroad. There, in 1869, the president of the Central Pacific Railroad drove a gold spike to link the tracks laid by his company with those of the Union Pacific Railroad.

Arches National Park

Images etched on Newspaper Rock hold clues to the ancient life of the Anasazi.

Timeline

1776
Silvestre Velez de Escalante and Francisco Atanasio Dominguez explore Utah

1824
Jim Bridger comes upon Great Salt Lake

1846
Donner-Reed party crosses Utah; nearly half the party later dies

1847
First Mormons arrive

1848
Mexico cedes Utah to U.S.

1850
Congress creates Utah Territory

1867
Mormon Tabernacle completed

1875
Brigham Young Academy established; later becomes BYU

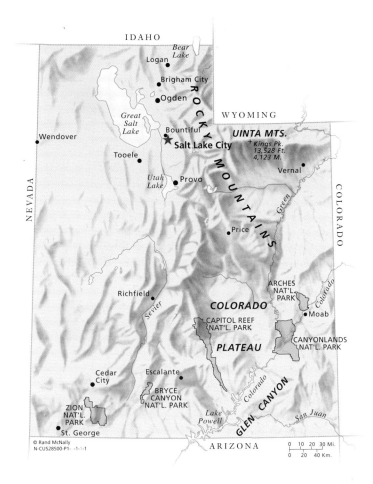

© Rand McNally
N-CUS28500-P1- -1-1-1

Park City, in the mountains east of Salt Lake City, is famous for its ski resorts.

People, Places, and Economy

About 70 percent of Utah's people are Mormon. Salt Lake City is home to the world headquarters of their church. Temple Square features the spired Mormon Temple and the Mormon Tabernacle, famous for its choir. The people of Utah have developed a diversified economy. Many work in service industries, including tourism and skiing. Other Utah workers manufacture products such as aerospace-, defense-, and computer-related items. Mining and agriculture are traditional activities that still contribute to Utah's economy.

The Way It Was . . . The Mormons

Brigham Young on the shores of the Great Salt Lake

After the founding of their church in New York in 1830, the Mormons were persecuted wherever they settled. When the church's founder, Joseph Smith, was murdered by a mob in Illinois in 1844, the Mormons knew they had to move once again. Their new leader, Brigham Young, studied surveys of the West, searching for a place where the Mormons could practice their religion in peace. Soon an advance party led by Young began the long trek west. They arrived at the Great Salt Lake in July 1847. To raise crops in the desert, they developed a system of irrigation channels. Then, in 1848, disaster struck. Swarms of grasshoppers threatened to destroy the crops that the pioneers had worked so hard to grow. The people were saved from starvation when sea gulls from the Great Salt Lake ate the grasshoppers. Today Seagull Monument, a column topped by golden statues of two sea gulls, stands in Salt Lake City.

State Facts

Utah Flag

American Seagull

Sego Lily

Blue Spruce

Nickname
Beehive State

Capital
Salt Lake City

Area
82,144 square miles
(212,752 sq km)
Rank: 12th

Population
2,389,000
Rank: 34th

Statehood
January 4, 1896
45th state admitted

Principal Rivers
Colorado River,
Green River

Highest Point
Kings Peak,
13,528 feet (4,123 m)

Motto
Industry

Song
"Utah, We Love Thee"

Famous People
Butch Cassidy,
Orrin G. Hatch,
Donny and Marie
Osmond,
Steve Young

1913
Strawberry River reservoir project completed

1952
Uranium deposits discovered near Moab

1996
Utah celebrates its centennial

2002
Salt Lake City hosts Winter Olympics

100 YEARS

1896
Utah becomes 45th state

1914
Capitol at Salt Lake City completed

1964
Flaming Gorge Dam on Green River completed

1982
Nation's first artificial heart operation completed at University of Utah Medical Center

2001
Jell-O® becomes official state snack

VERMONT

Vermont owes its name to the French explorer Samuel de Champlain. He dubbed the region *Vert Mont*, which is French for "green mountain." The name could not be more appropriate. The heavily forested Green Mountains run from north to south through the center of the state. In spring and summer, Vermont is covered by a blanket of lush greenery. In autumn, the blanket becomes a patchwork quilt of yellow, orange, purple, and red as the leaves of

deciduous trees change color. Winter brings another change as generous snowfalls transform the state into a wonderland of white.

Rolling Hills and Small Towns

Vermont is a mostly rural state. It has no large cities; instead, small towns and farms are scattered across the beautiful rolling landscape. Vermont's lack of urban development is partly due to the fact that it is the only New England state without a seacoast. Thus, Vermont never developed seaports or a shipping industry. Most Vermonters want to keep the state the way it is. They have passed strong state laws to protect the environment and to control construction.

The town of East Corinth, nestled in the hills of eastern Vermont

Trees are tapped to produce maple syrup.

Vermont's Economy

Many of Vermont's main economic activities and products are tied closely to the land. Understandably, wood is an important product in a state that is three-fourths forest. Dairy farms are also common, especially near Lake Champlain. Vermont has the largest granite quarries in the United States and is also a major producer of marble. The state's scenery and outdoor recreational opportunities make it a thriving center of tourism. For example, the mountains, long winters, and deep snows attract flocks of skiers. And people from around the country travel to Vermont to witness the brilliant colors of fall.

Timeline

1609
Samuel de Champlain claims Vermont for France

1666
Fort St. Anne built by French

1724
Fort Dummer (now Brattleboro), first permanent European settlement in Vermont, established

1770
Green Mountain Boys drive New York settlers from Vermont

1775
Ethan Allen and Green Mountain Boys capture Fort Ticonderoga

1777
Vermont declares itself an independent republic

1791
Vermont becomes 14th state

1805
Montpelier becomes state capital

1896
Vermont becomes first state to allow absentee voting

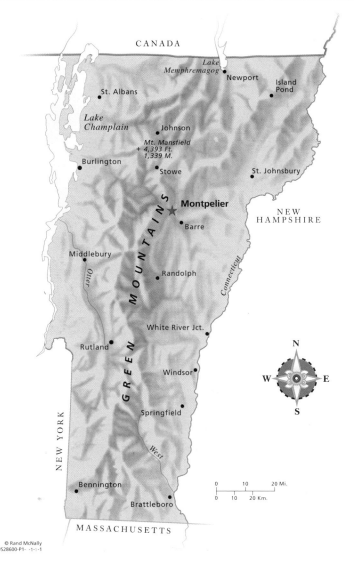

CANADA

Lake
Memphremagog • Newport

St. Albans • Island
Pond

Lake
Champlain

Johnson •

Mt. Mansfield
+ 4,393 Ft.
1,339 M.

Burlington •

• Stowe St. Johnsbury •

★ **Montpelier**

• Barre NEW
HAMPSHIRE

Middlebury •

Randolph •

Otter

Connecticut

White River Jct.

Rutland •

Windsor •

N

W • E

S

Springfield •

West

NEW YORK

Bennington •

0   10   20 Mi.
0 10   20 Km.

Brattleboro •

© Rand McNally
N-CUS28600-P1- -1-1-1

MASSACHUSETTS

GREEN MOUNTAINS

© Rand McNally
N-CUS28600-P1- -1-1-1

*Syrup production has changed
very little since the 1800s.*

The Way It Was . . . Maple Syrup

Early spring in Vermont is
sugaring time. That's when
millions of sugar maple trees
are tapped to collect the sweet
sap that becomes maple syrup.
Native Americans had the idea
first. They caught the sap in
bark buckets. Then they placed
hot stones in the sap to boil
off the water. What remained
was thick, sweet maple syrup.
Today's syrup producers use
modern equipment, but the
basic process is the same. The
sap from four trees (about 40
gallons, or 150 liters, of sap)
must be boiled down to
produce one gallon (about four
liters) of syrup. As the leading
maple syrup producer in the
United States, Vermont makes
more than 500,000 gallons
(1,890,000 liters) of delicious
syrup each year.

One of Vermont's many covered bridges spans a quiet stream.

The Town Meeting

In Vermont's towns, people govern themselves much as they did
in colonial times — through town meetings. At a town meeting,
citizens gather at the town hall to discuss issues and vote on
them directly, without the use of representatives. Such meetings,
in which communities make governmental decisions according
to majority rule, are the purest form of democracy.

1923
Calvin Coolidge
becomes president

1934
First ski tow in U.S.
built at Woodstock

1970
Environmental Control
Law passed

1991
Vermont celebrates
its bicentennial

1911
Vermont estab-
lishes first state
tourism bureau

1927
River flooding causes 60
deaths and millions of
dollars in damage

1965
First Head
Start program

1978
Ben & Jerry's Homemade
ice cream company founded
in Burlington

2005
Howard Dean elected
chair of Democratic
National Committee

VIRGINIA

This southern state on the Atlantic Ocean was named after Queen Elizabeth I of England, the "Virgin Queen." Virginia is called the Mother of Presidents because it is the birthplace of eight United States presidents — more than any other state. "Mother of States" is another Virginia nickname, due to the fact that eight other states were formed from land that was once part of Virginia. One of the original 13 colonies, Virginia has served as a backdrop for many dramatic moments in United States history.

Thomas Jefferson designed his mountaintop home, Monticello.

A State Steeped in History

The first permanent English settlement in what is now the United States was Jamestown, founded in 1607. Many important historical figures called Virginia home: Patrick Henry, who uttered the famous words "Give me liberty or give me death" in 1775; Thomas Jefferson, writer of the Declaration of Independence and the third president of the United States; James Madison, chief writer of the United States Constitution and the fourth president; and George Washington, the first president.

Natural Beauty

Virginia's spectacular scenery includes the Blue Ridge Mountains and, to the northwest, the Shenandoah Valley. This valley is 150 miles (240 kilometers) long and covered by pastures, crop fields, orchards, and vineyards. Toward the southern end of the valley is Natural Bridge, a limestone arch that reaches a height of 215 feet (65 meters). George Washington is said to have climbed the arch and marked his initials on it. In the east, along the Atlantic Ocean, Virginia has lovely islands and long, sandy beaches such as Virginia Beach, a popular vacation destination.

Mount Vernon, near Alexandria, was home to George Washington.

The beautiful Shenandoah National Park

Timeline

1612
Tobacco first cultivated by colonists

1732
George Washington born in Westmoreland County

1780
Richmond becomes capital of commonwealth

1607
Jamestown founded by English settlers

1693
College of William and Mary founded in Williamsburg

1776
Virginia adopts its first constitution, becomes an independent commonwealth

1781
Benedict Arnold burns Richmond and Petersburg for British

MARYLAND

Winchester
Potomac
Washington, D.C.
Arlington
Front Royal
Alexandria
Shenandoah
Harrisonburg
SHENANDOAH NAT'L. PARK
Fredericksburg
Staunton
Waynesboro
Charlottesville
Rappahannock
Covington
Lexington
James
Richmond
WEST VIRGINIA
Potomac
Chesapeake Bay
DELMARVA PEN.
ASSATEAGUE I.
CHINCOTEAGUE I.
PARRAMORE I.
HOG I.
Lynchburg
Hopewell
York
KENTUCKY
Roanoke
Bedford
Appomattox
Blacksburg
BLUE RIDGE
Williamsburg
SMITH I.
Bluefield
Petersburg
Jamestown
ATLANTIC
Clinch
Newport News
Norfolk
OCEAN
Wytheville
Smith Mtn. Lake
John H. Kerr Reservoir
Portsmouth
Virginia Beach
Bristol
APPALACHIAN
Roanoke
TENNESSEE
Mt. Rogers 5,729 Ft. 1,746 M.
Martinsville
Danville
NORTH CAROLINA

N W E S

0 10 20 30 Mi.
0 20 40 Km.

McNally 8700-P1- -1-1-1

Virginia's Diverse Economy

Virginia's chief crops include tobacco, hay, corn, soybeans, peanuts, dairy products, and beef cattle. However, agriculture represents only a small part of the state's economy. Tourism is big business in Virginia, which is home to more historical sites than any other state. The federal government also plays a major role, with many government agencies and military bases located in Virginia. In the area of manufacturing, Virginia's leading products include ships, chemicals, and printed materials.

Appomattox Court House, where the Civil War came to an end

Changing of the Guard at the Tomb of the Unknowns

The Way It Was...
Arlington National Cemetery

Arlington National Cemetery is one of the most famous cemeteries in the world. It occupies land that once belonged to Mary Custis Lee and her husband Robert E. Lee. When the Civil War began, Robert became a general in the Confederate Army, and the Lees had to leave their mansion, which was called Arlington House. Union troops soon arrived and used Arlington House as a headquarters. Later, the federal government confiscated the land from the Lees and made part of it a military cemetery. Today the cemetery is the final resting place of many Americans who served their country in times of war. A torch burns day and night over the grave of assassinated United States President John F. Kennedy, who was buried in the cemetery in 1963.

Ships at Newport News, a busy seaport

State Facts

Virginia Flag

Cardinal

Dogwood Blossom

Dogwood

Nickname
Old Dominion

Capital
Richmond

Area
39,594 square miles (102,548 sq km)
Rank: 37th

Population
7,459,800
Rank: 12th

Statehood
June 25, 1788
10th state admitted

Principal Rivers
James River, Potomac River, Rappahannock River

Highest Point
Mount Rogers, 5,729 feet (1,746 m)

Motto
Sic semper tyrannis
(Thus always to tyrants)

Song
"Carry Me Back to Old Virginia"

Famous People
Arthur Ashe, Willa Cather, Patrick Henry, Thomas Jefferson, Robert E. Lee, James Madison, Pocahontas, George Washington, Woodrow Wilson

1788
Virginia becomes 10th state

1861
Virginia secedes from Union

1870
Virginia reenters Union

1964
Chesapeake Bay Bridge-Tunnel completed

2003
Hurricane Isabel causes more than $1 billion damage

1781
British surrender at Yorktown; last major battle of Revolutionary War

1819
University of Virginia founded by Thomas Jefferson

1865
Confederate forces surrender at Appomattox Court House, ending Civil War

1912
Woodrow Wilson elected president

1989
L. Douglas Wilder becomes the first African American elected governor of a state

WASHINGTON

Majestic Mt. Rainier

Wealth from Resources

Commercial boats catch large numbers of salmon, steelhead trout, and other fish off Washington's coast. The depth of Puget Sound makes it a fine harbor for large ships, which in turn have allowed cities like Seattle and Tacoma to become major ports. Vast stands of trees make Washington one of the leading states in the timber industry, ahead of Oregon in terms of the amount of wood removed from forests each year. Washington is also the country's leading producer of apples and pears.

Washington, named for the country's first president, George Washington, is covered with lush forests of fir and other evergreen trees. The state is also known for its many magnificent mountains, the highest of which, Mount Rainier, rises in the Cascade Range. Moist winds from the Pacific Ocean bring a lot of rain — and in the mountains, a lot of snow — to western Washington. By the time the winds have crossed the Cascades, they have little moisture left. As a result, much of eastern Washington — on the other side of the mountains — has few trees and is desert-like.

Seattle's famous Pike Place Market is located near the waterfront.

Land and Water Wonders

Olympic National Park has mild-climate rain forests, which are not found anywhere else in the United States. The forests consist mainly of Sitka spruce, western hemlock, western red cedar, and Douglas fir. Washington sparkles with numerous rivers, waterfalls, and lakes. Although some lakes were formed by the action of glaciers, the state's largest lake, Franklin D. Roosevelt Lake, was formed by the Grand Coulee Dam.

A lone barn is surrounded by fields of wheat in eastern Washington.

Timeline

1775
Bruno Heceta lands in Washington

1791
Colony established on Neah Bay

1805
Meriwether Lewis and William Clark reach Washington

1810
British-Canadian trading post established near Spokane

1811
First American settlement, Fort Okanogan, established

1836
Marcus Whitman establishes mission near present-day Walla Walla

1846
Oregon Treaty sets Washington's boundaries

1852
Gold discovered at Fort Colville

1853
Congress creates Washington Territory

Logging is an important part of Washington's economy.

Seattle's Attractions

The Seattle area is home to companies that make aircraft and aerospace equipment, computers and computer software, and other high-tech products. People can enjoy spectacular views of Seattle and nearby mountains from the Space Needle, a 607-foot (185-meter) observation tower. It was built for the World's Fair held in Seattle in 1962. The Space Needle and other fair buildings make up Seattle Center, which includes theaters and a science museum. A monorail built for the fair still carries people to Seattle Center.

The Way It Was . . . Mount St. Helens

The peaceful beauty of Washington's southern Cascade Mountains was shattered on the morning of May 18, 1980, when Mount St. Helens suddenly erupted. The volcano's peak was blasted away, leaving Mount St. Helens about 1,300 feet (394 meters) shorter than before. Fifty-seven people and an unknown number of wild animals were killed. Hot rock and ash spewed by the volcano melted the mountain snow, causing floods and mud slides. In all, southwestern Washington suffered billions of dollars in damage. In 1982 Congress created the Mount St. Helens National Volcanic Monument, the first of its kind. Protected by the United States Forest Service, the area within the monument is gradually renewing itself. However, Mount St. Helens has had hundreds of small eruptions since 1980, and scientists expect the eruptions to continue.

Explosive Mount St. Helens

1855
Waves of settlers
begin arriving

1883
Northern Pacific
Railroad reaches
Puget Sound

1889
Washington becomes
42nd state

1942
Grand
Coulee Dam
completed

1962
Century 21 World's
Fair held in Seattle

1980
Mount St.
Helens erupts

1990
Goodwill Games held in
Spokane and Seattle

1993
National summit held to
address concerns of loggers
and environmentalists

1996
Gary Locke elected first
Chinese American U.S. governor

WEST VIRGINIA

Until the Civil War, West Virginia was part of the state of Virginia. Residents of Virginia's northwestern counties wanted to fight for the Union side in the war, while the rest of Virginia's residents wanted to fight for the Confederacy. The northwestern counties pulled away from Virginia in 1861 and became a state in 1863 as the Civil War raged on. Most of West Virginia's land is mountainous, and many West Virginians make their living from under the mountain rocks: Coal mining is a big

business in the state. West Virginia is also known for manufacturing glass. Many of the glass marbles that kids play with come from the town of Parkersburg.

Spruce Knob, located in the Monongahela National Forest, soars above colorful autumn trees.

Natural Beauty

Rugged mountains, thick forests, and babbling waters are just a few of the reasons that tourists flock to West Virginia. Many people enjoy white-water rafting on such rivers as the Cheat and the New. The New River Gorge, known as the Grand Canyon of the East, is home to one of the largest natural arched rock bridges in the world. West Virginia also has about 200 natural hot springs that attract bathers.

Grave Creek Mound

Grave Creek Mound, in Moundsville, south of Wheeling, is one of the largest prehistoric burial mounds in the United States. The cone-shaped mound is 62 feet (19 meters) high and 240 feet (73 meters) in diameter. Inside the mound, archaeologists have found tools and stones covered with markings. It is estimated that the mound took more than 100 years to build. Today a museum houses the tools and other artifacts found there. These artifacts have helped archaeologists find out more about the people who lived in West Virginia thousands of years ago.

Harpers Ferry

Coal mining equipment

Timeline

1669 John Lederer explores region

1727 Settlement established at New Mecklenburg (now Shepherdstown)

1742 Coal discovered on Coal River

1782 British and Native Americans invade Fort Henry

1788 Charleston founded

1836 B&O Railroad reaches Harpers Ferry

1859 John Brown hanged after unsuccessful raid at Harpers Ferry

1860 Beginning of famous feud between Hatfield and McCoy families

Weirton

Wheeling

PENNSYLVANIA

OHIO

Ohio

Parkersburg

Fairmont

Morgantown

MARYLAND

Cumberland

Keyser

Martinsburg
Shepherdstown

Harpers
Ferry

Clarksburg

Blackwater Falls
State Park ■

Weston

Elkins

Potomac

+ Spruce Knob
4,861 Ft.
1,482 M.

Cheat

Potomac

Point Pleasant

Kanawha

★ Charleston

Huntington

Richwood

VIRGINIA

New

Guyandotte

Oak
Hill

Williamson

Beckley

Greenbrier

N
W E
S

Tug Fork

KENTUCKY

Princeton

Bluefield

© Rand McNally
N-CUS28900-P1- -1-1-1

ALLEGHENY PLATEAU

APPALACHIAN MOUNTAINS

0   10   20 Mi.
0 10 20 30 Km.

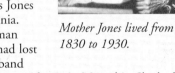

Bluegrass band performs
in West Virginia

John Brown's Attempt to End Slavery

John Brown was a white man who was born in 1800, when slavery was common in parts of the United States. Brown felt that slavery was wrong and that it should be outlawed. In 1859, Brown and several of his followers decided to steal weapons from the federal armory at Harpers Ferry and give the weapons to slaves. They hoped that the slaves would begin a revolt that would end slavery. However, federal troops attacked Brown and his supporters at the armory, killing two of Brown's sons. Brown was later tried, convicted, and hanged for his part in the plan.

The Way It Was . . . "Mother" Jones

In the 1890s, Mary Harris Jones came to live in West Virginia. A small, white-haired woman in her early sixties, Jones had lost her four children and husband during the 1867 yellow fever epidemic in Memphis. She had tried to rebuild her life as a dressmaker in Chicago, but her business was destroyed in the Great Chicago Fire of 1871. When Jones arrived in West Virginia, she saw that people were laboring long hours for little money in factories and coal mines. Jones hated to see this injustice, and struggled to help workers gain better working conditions and wages. Grateful workers called her "Mother." Jones was jailed several times for leading labor strikes. She even was jailed for three months when she was 83 years old. Jones died after her 100th birthday, but the work she did for laborers lives on.

Mother Jones lived from 1830 to 1930.

1863
West Virginia becomes 35th state

1872
State constitution ratified

1890
United Mine Workers of America union begins organizing West Virginia coal miners

1907
Mine accident at Monongah kills 361

1954
West Virginia Turnpike opens

1959
National Radio Astronomy Observatory opens

1972
Buffalo Creek flood kills more than 100

1984
Mary Lou Retton wins Olympic gold medal in gymnastics

2003
American prisoner of war Jessica Lynch rescued in Iraq

WISCONSIN

The rivers, lakes, and forests of northern Wisconsin draw thousands of outdoor enthusiasts.

A marina on the Milwaukee River offers views of downtown buildings.

Visiting Wisconsin

Wisconsin's scenic beauty and outdoor recreational opportunities help make it a top vacation destination, especially for people who live in other midwestern states. For example, the state's many lakes and rivers offer excellent fishing in both summer and winter. One especially busy tourist area is Door County, which offers a long lakeshore, picturesque towns, and numerous state parks. Another popular vacation spot is the Wisconsin Dells, a region of beautiful rock formations along the Wisconsin River.

The name *Wisconsin* comes from a Chippewa word that means "gathering of waters." The name is appropriate, for Wisconsin is bordered by water on three sides: Lake Michigan on the east, the Menominee and Brule Rivers and Lake Superior on the north, and the St. Croix and Mississippi Rivers on the west. The state contains 15,000 or so lakes and about 10,000 rivers and streams. Wisconsin also has a lot of dairy cows — more than any other state, in fact. Milk from these cows is used to make a variety of products. With more than 200 cheese factories, Wisconsin produces almost half the cheese eaten in the United States.

International Wisconsin

Many of Wisconsin's early settlers were from Germany and Scandinavia, and the influences of their cultures is still seen in Wisconsin. For example, at Little Norway, a town just outside Madison, visitors can see a Norwegian village as it would have looked in the 1800s. In Milwaukee, festivals such as Germanfest offer visitors the chance to eat delicious food and learn more about the diverse cultures that have contributed to Wisconsin's past and present.

Farms near Mt. Calvary

Timeline

1634 Jean Nicolet lands on Green Bay shore

1673 Jacques Marquette and Louis Jolliet travel through Wisconsin

1763 England receives Wisconsin from France

1783 Wisconsin becomes part of U.S.

1836 Congress creates the Wisconsin Territory

1848 Wisconsin becomes 30th state

1851 First Wisconsin state fair held

1854 Republican Party founded in Ripon

Duluth
Superior
Ashland
Lake Superior

MINNESOTA

MICHIGAN

Hayward

Brule

Rhinelander

Timms Hill
1,951 Ft.
595 M.

Menominee

Wausau

Marinette

Green Bay

Door Peninsula

Sturgeon Bay

Eau Claire

Marshfield

Stevens Point

Chippewa

Wisconsin Rapids

Black

Appleton

Green Bay

Petenwell Lake

Oshkosh

Lake Winnebago

Manitowoc

Mississippi

La Crosse

Wisconsin Dells

Fond du Lac

Sheboygan

Waupun

Baraboo

West Bend

Lake Michigan

Prairie du Chien

Wisconsin

MILITARY RIDGE

★ **Madison**

Milwaukee

Waukesha

IOWA

Platteville

Janesville

Racine

Dubuque

Beloit

Kenosha

ILLINOIS

© Rand McNally
N-CUS29000-P1- -1-1-1

0 10 20 Mi.
0 10 20 30 Km.

The Birkebeiner ski race is a popular annual event.

State Facts

WISCONSIN
1848
Wisconsin Flag

Robin

Wood Violet

Sugar Maple

Nickname
Badger State

Capital
Madison

Area
54,310 square miles
(140,662 sq km)
Rank: 25th

Population
5,509,000
Rank: 20th

Statehood
May 29, 1848
30th state admitted

Principal Rivers
Mississippi River,
Wisconsin River

Highest Point
Timms Hill,
1,951 feet (595 m)

Motto
Forward

Song
"On, Wisconsin!"

Famous People
Chris Farley,
Harry Houdini,
Robert M. La Follette,
Donald K. "Deke" Slayton,
Laura Ingalls Wilder,
Frank Lloyd Wright

RINGLING BROS ARENIC SENSATION

MAY WIRTH
WORLD FAMOUS EQUESTRIENNE
THE GREATEST BARE BACK RIDER THAT EVER LIVED

An early poster advertising a Ringling Brothers circus

The Way It Was...
The Circus Is in Town!

In 1884, five brothers from Baraboo decided to put on a circus near their hometown. The brothers paraded through Baraboo playing musical instruments, hoping to get people interested in their show. Only 52 people came to their first performance, but the Ringling brothers were not discouraged. Two years later, after touring with and learning from other circuses, they put on another of their own shows. This circus featured tumblers, magicians, and music but had only a few animals — a pet pig and a few snakes. Gradually, the circus became larger, and the brothers gave up performing in order to manage the business side of the circus. Today Baraboo is home to the Circus World Museum, where visitors can go "under the big top" to learn the history of American circuses.

The Badger State

In the early decades of the 1800s, southwestern Wisconsin experienced a lead rush. During the rush, miners staked their claims quickly, with little thought for shelter. When winter came, some miners simply dug caves in the sides of hills. These temporary quarters resembled the burrows that badgers dig, and so people began calling the miners "badgers." These independent and hardworking men became a symbol of Wisconsin, which modern-day residents proudly call the Badger State.

A
B
C

1856
Nation's first kindergarten opens in Watertown

1871
Peshtigo forest fire kills 1,200

1884
Ringling brothers start their circus in Baraboo

1917
State Capitol completed in Madison

1970
Earth Day started by Senator Gaylord Nelson

1997
Green Bay Packers win Super Bowl

2001
Governor Tommy Thompson appointed U.S. Secretary of Health and Human Services

WYOMING

The Grand Tetons

In rugged, beautiful Wyoming, the dry grasslands of the Great Plains bump up against the snowcapped peaks of the Rocky Mountains. Even today, Wyoming's wide-open spaces are largely unspoiled by humans — Wyoming has fewer residents than any other state but is ranked ninth in amount of land. Visitors to Wyoming delight in catching sight of the state's many wild animals, which include elk, antelope, moose, buffalo, deer, coyotes, bears, bobcats, mountain lions, and eagles. Wyoming's name comes from the Delaware Indian word meaning "on the great plain."

Scenic Wonders

Yellowstone National Park, located mostly within Wyoming, is best known for its dozens of geysers. The most famous Yellowstone geyser is Old Faithful. It erupts every 76 minutes on average, spewing boiling-hot water more than 100 feet (30 meters) into the air. In northeastern Wyoming, Devils Tower National Monument, the country's first national monument, features an imposing column of volcanic rock 865 feet (262 meters) high.

Economic Wealth

Wyoming is a leading producer of oil, natural gas, and coal. The state also produces the lesser known, yet still important, minerals bentonite and trona. Bentonite is used chiefly in the oil-drilling industry, and trona is used in making glass. Wyoming ranchers raise beef cattle and sheep. Crops grown in Wyoming include hay, sugar beets, barley, and wheat. The United States government owns almost half the land in the state. In addition to national parks, this land is used for grazing, mining, logging, and military activities.

The Sinclair Oil refinery

Old Faithful

Timeline

1743
Francois and Louis Joseph de la Verendrye explore Wyoming

1803
Eastern Wyoming becomes part of U.S. through Louisiana Purchase

1807
John Colter travels through present-day Yellowstone Park

1834
William Sublette and Robert Campbell establish Fort William

1867
City of Cheyenne founded

1868
Congress creates Territory of Wyoming

1869
Union Pacific Railroad crosses state

1872
Yellowstone becomes first national park in the U.S.

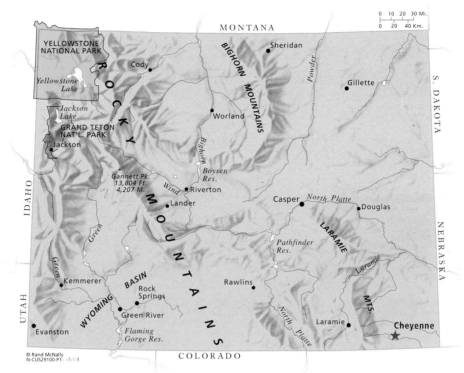

A bull rider holds on tight at Cheyenne Frontier Days.

State Facts

Wyoming Flag

Meadowlark

Indian Paintbrush

Cottonwood

Nickname
Equality State

Capital
Cheyenne

Area
97,100 square miles
(251,488 sq km)
Rank: 9th

Population
506,500
Rank: 50th

Statehood
July 10, 1890
44th state admitted

Principal Rivers
Bighorn River,
Green River,
North Platte River

Highest Point
Gannett Peak,
13,804 feet (4,207 m)

Motto
Equal rights

Song
"Wyoming"

Famous People
Richard B. Cheney,
Curt Gowdy,
Jackson Pollock,
Nellie Tayloe Ross,
Spotted Tail

Frontier Culture

Wyoming celebrates its heritage during Frontier Days, held in Cheyenne each July since 1897. The ten-day festival includes a rodeo, in which prizes are awarded for such skills as calf-roping and bronco riding. Many other towns in Wyoming also hold rodeos, but these cowboy events are not the only reminders of Wyoming's frontier past. Even today there are visible ruts along the former Oregon Trail. These deep grooves were created by wagon wheels and oxen hooves, as thousands of settlers headed west across Wyoming.

The Way It Was . . . Dinosaur Battleground

Edward Drinker Cope

Back in the Jurassic period, some of the world's largest dinosaurs roamed the area that is now Wyoming. In 1877, Union Pacific railroad workers found dinosaur bones near Como Bluff in southeastern Wyoming. This area contained so many bones that a local sheepherder had used them to build a cabin. Othneil Charles Marsh and Edward Drinker Cope, two important paleontologists, learned about Como Bluff but were not willing to dig together. Soon the two men's crews were ruining each other's work and stealing each other's workers. Despite this bone battle, the expeditions found nearly complete skeletons of *Allosaurus*, *Camptosaurus*, *Diplodocus*, *Stegosaurus*, and many others. Boxcars of bones rode the Union Pacific rails to faraway eastern museums to be put on display. From Como Bluff alone came 26 previously unknown dinosaur species and 45 skeletons of Jurassic mammals.

1890
Wyoming becomes 44th state

1906
Devils Tower named first national monument in U.S.

1988
Wildfires ravage Yellowstone National Park

1995
Wolves reintroduced to Yellowstone National Park

1886
University of Wyoming founded

1892
Johnson County Cattle War

1929
Opening of Grand Teton National Park

1947
F. E. Warren Air Force Base opens near Cheyenne

1978
World's first large computer-controlled telescope built at Jelm Mountain

1990
Wyoming celebrates its 100th birthday

2004
Richard B. Cheney elected to second term as U.S. vice president

Index of Major Places on the Maps